T0352978

BADASS
ANCESTORS

© Aaron Werner/Werner Entertainment

About the Author

Patti Wigington has been a practicing Pagan and witch since 1987, and is licensed clergy in her home state of Ohio, where she works as an educator in her local Pagan community. She is the High Priestess and founder of Clan of the Stone Circle, a Celtic Pagan tradition. In 2007, Patti joined LearnReligions.com, formerly About.com, as their Paganism and Wicca expert. She has a B.A. in History and is the author of several novels and a children's book, as well as *The Good Witch's Daily Spell Book, Wicca Practical Magic,* and *The Daily Spell Journal.* She shares her home with a pair of college students, a few dozen Tarot decks, lots of dead relatives, and a very large dog. You can find Patti online at www.pattiwigington.com.

PATTI WIGINGTON

BADASS
ANCESTORS

Finding Your Power with Ancestral Guides

Llewellyn Publications
Woodbury, Minnesota

Badass Ancestors: Finding Your Power with Ancestral Guides © 2020 by Patti Wigington. All rights reserved. No part of this book may be used or reproduced in any manner whatsoever, including internet usage, without written permission from Llewellyn Publications, except in the case of brief quotations embodied in critical articles and reviews.

FIRST EDITION
Sixth Printing, 2023

Book design by Samantha Penn
Cover design by Shira Atakpu
Editing by Laura Kurtz

Llewellyn Publications is a registered trademark of Llewellyn Worldwide Ltd.

Library of Congress Cataloging-in-Publication Data
Names: Wigington, Patti, author.
Title: Badass ancestors : finding your power with ancestral guides / by
   Patti Wigington.
Description: First edition. | Woodbury, Minnesota : Llewellyn Publications,
   [2020] | Includes bibliographical references and index. | Summary:
   "Ancestor veneration, includes geneaology tips, spells, recipes,
   exercises"-- Provided by publisher.
Identifiers: LCCN 2020028159 (print) | LCCN 2020028160 (ebook) | ISBN
   9780738764986 (paperback) | ISBN 9780738765167 (ebook)
Subjects: LCSH: Ancestor worship. | Genealogy--Religious aspects. | Rites
   and ceremonies. | Divination. | Spirituality.
Classification: LCC BL467 .W54 2020 (print) | LCC BL467 (ebook) | DDC
   202/.13--dc23
LC record available at https://lccn.loc.gov/2020028159
LC ebook record available at https://lccn.loc.gov/2020028160

Llewellyn Worldwide Ltd. does not participate in, endorse, or have any authority or responsibility concerning private business transactions between our authors and the public.

All mail addressed to the author is forwarded but the publisher cannot, unless specifically instructed by the author, give out an address or phone number.

Any internet references contained in this work are current at publication time, but the publisher cannot guarantee that a specific location will continue to be maintained. Please refer to the publisher's website for links to authors' websites and other sources.

Llewellyn Publications
A Division of Llewellyn Worldwide Ltd.
2143 Wooddale Drive
Woodbury, MN 55125-2989
www.llewellyn.com

Printed in the United States of America

Other Books by Patti Wigington

The Good Witch's Daily Spell Book

Wicca Practical Magic

The Daily Spell Book

Herb Magic: An Introduction to Magical Herbalism and Spells

Forthcoming Books by Patti Wigington

Healing Witchcraft: Spells, Rituals,
and Wisdom for Radical Self-Care

For Barrett, who makes me want to be a
badass ancestor myself someday.

CONTENTS

Introduction   1

One: Ancestor Veneration Around the World   11

Two: Finding Your Badass Kin—Genealogy 101   25

Three: Your Badass Ancestor Altar   61

Four: Working with Your Badass Family   83

Five: Rituals and Meditations for Your Kin   103

Six: Problem Ancestors—You Can't Choose Your People   127

Seven: Badass Ancestors of the Heart   139

Eight: Connecting to Archetypal Badasses   147

Nine: Divination with Your Badass Kin   167

Ten: Eating with Your Ancestors   183

Eleven: Your Badass Legacy   199

Conclusion: Putting It All Together   215

Appendix: Genealogy Resources   219

Bibliography   229

Index   233

INTRODUCTION

You can't choose your family.

How often have you heard that old chestnut? It's true, though—while you get to pick your friend circle, your romantic partners, and your coworkers to some degree, you've got no choice when it comes to your kinfolk. When it comes to relatives, you're stuck with the luck of a random draw. Most of the people whose DNA runs through you have been dead for generations, and all of them—both the living and those who have crossed over the veil—have their own unique quirks, flaws, and personality traits. By learning to work with your ancestral guides, you can build up your own sense of personal empowerment.

Empowerment is a big word with a lot of different meanings, and it's one that more and more people are embracing. But what exactly does empowerment mean to you personally? Maybe it's a chance to feel like you're in charge of your life and the things that happen to you. Perhaps you want to feel more involved in how you respond and react to the people and events in the world around you. Or just possibly, you want to feel like you can handle any curveball life throws at you and be stronger emotionally, physically, and spiritually.

1

For some people, working with ancestral guides is a way to heal from trauma. They say that trauma can be passed through generations; if that's the case, then certainly healing can be as well. Why not call upon your ancestors to help you navigate the murky waters of recovery, self-guidance, and wellness? If your ancestors themselves were the cause of the trauma, you can break the cycle of suffering by interacting with them. After all, if unpleasantness runs in your family, isn't it about time for it to run out? We can't change the past, but we sure can face it head on and refuse to let it define us.

You can also work with your relations for assistance in mundane, material things. You might petition them for protection, requesting them to watch over you in times of trouble. Try asking them to help out with things like financial matters. For example, do you have a dream of buying yourself a house or opening your own business? That's where your ancestors may just be able to step in and intervene—by embracing their power, we allow ourselves to develop our own.

Have you ever really thought about who your people were and where they came from? Some of them did wonderful things … and let's not kid ourselves, some of them were pretty unpleasant. But all of them can be called upon to tap into our inner strength, help us set boundaries, and find wisdom and guidance when we need it the most.

So how do we do that, exactly? We all want to find our power and feel like we're in control of our own futures but have sort of forgotten how. Let's face it, we're *busy*. There are plenty of us who feel we've lost our connection to the sacred. More specifically, while we *try* to embody sacred principles, we find ourselves failing miserably, and then beating ourselves up over it. In fact, we often judge ourselves against the standards of our forebears.

Great-grandma drove a munitions jeep in World War II. Uncle Bill fought in Vietnam. Great-great-aunt so-and-so rode across the prairie in a covered wagon and survived cholera three times on the Oregon Trail. What on earth would they think of us, knowing that we're one broken shoelace away from a complete breakdown simply because we forgot that one of our kids had soccer practice Tuesday night at five?

If your ancestors are anything like mine, they'd probably tell you to sit down, be quiet, have a nice hot cup of pity-party tea (probably spiked with bourbon), and then get your act together. *Chin up, kids!*

For many of us, finding that sense of personal power that our ancestors had can be a challenge, thanks to modern society's time constraints and the never-ending demands on our schedules. As mentioned earlier, we're busy—women, particularly, but men as well—focusing on other people. We're raising children, making sure our romantic partners are getting their needs met, caring for aging parents, and doing the emotional labor for our families and households. We're working full-time and we find ourselves under constant pressure to do more, to be more. We live in a world that is constantly reminding us that, for whatever reasons, we're just not good enough no matter what. *Lose weight, gain weight, wear more makeup, wear less makeup, stay home with your kids, go have a career.*

Yet, for thousands of years, people have managed to live through far more stressful situations than delivering a kid late to kindergarten, breaking a nail, or double-booking meetings at work. Our ancestors were survivors of things far more frightening than our first-world problems. They were *strong.* How do we know that? Because you're here. Your bloodline survived millennia of plague, war, pestilence, famine, infant mortality, and just plain old bad luck … just to make *you.*

That means your ancestors were badasses.

I started researching my own family history more than thirty years ago, back in the days when you couldn't just hop online, plug a name into a search engine, and come back with thousands of results. This was the late eighties, when genealogy research involved writing letters to old ladies in dusty archives somewhere and hoping that in a few months your self-addressed stamped envelope (many people don't even remember what those are) would come back with a copy of a marriage certificate from the nineteenth century. More often than not, it didn't, because she couldn't find it ... and then you started the process all over again, writing to a different little old lady in a different dusty archive two counties over.

Over the past three decades, I've uncovered a lot of different types of people. From criminals to kings, from sinners to literal saints, they're all connected to me, either by blood or marriage. I'll be the first to admit that some of them are problematic for me. A few of my people were wealthy landowners in colonial Virginia, which entails everything you're thinking it does. It's been an uncomfortable truth to acknowledge that people in my bloodline enslaved other human beings, but it's a fact and is unavoidable.

In 1892, my great-something grandfather killed his wife and then himself in an alcohol-fueled fit of "temporary insanity," or at least that's what the newspapers said the coroner's inquest verdict was. That one was kept quiet for a long time, and I learned about it when my great-grandmother blurted it out one night at dinner, much to the abject shock and horror of my great-grandfather, who was the grandson of the deceased couple.

I've got another distant connection who sailed down the Ohio River in 1797 to make the Kentucky frontier safe for white settlers and in doing so, earned himself the nickname "Indian Bill" because he took so many Native scalps. A few more did awful things during the years immediately following the Civil War. A couple of other far-off cousinly connections made their way out to the Old West and became famous gunslingers; there are mixed reviews about their penchants for shooting those who caused them offense.

These are problem ancestors for me—but they're mine. It's pretty much a guarantee that you'll encounter some of your own as well, and we'll talk later about how to deal with these types of people when doing spiritual ancestor work. But keep in mind that in addition to the kinfolk who did Really Bad Things, there are also plenty who did some wonderful stuff.

I've found people who were brave and heroic: a handful of Revolutionary War soldiers; women who survived plagues, famine, and the endless cycles of childbirth and nursing and keeping families together; doctors and dentists and sailors and artists and inventors and teachers and a king who was so popular he later got canonized as a saint; immigrants from Western Europe and England and Ireland who ended up in Chicago to work as laborers, blacksmiths, and cabinetmakers; Scottish freedom fighters, as well as a couple of Frenchmen who tried to kill an unjust king; Huguenots who fled religious persecution and made their way to the New World; and Quakers who fought for the abolition of slavery. My grandfather, one of the funniest people I've ever met in my life, was a scout pilot in World War II and told great stories about his wartime adventures in Europe. I claim all of them, with all of their many facets, good and bad alike.

What—or who—do we mean when talking about ancestors, exactly? There are different types. Familial ancestors are part of our family, the badasses who came before us somewhere in our family tree. They are your grandparents, your great-grandparents, even your extended network of aunts, uncles, and cousins. They are the people who by virtue of either bloodline, marriage, fosterage, or adoption are your family. If you consider someone your ancestor, whether they're in your direct line or part of the outward-reaching spiderweb of your family DNA, then for the purposes of this book, they're your ancestor.

There are also archetypal ancestors, who may or may not be genetically related to us but share a kinship with us as archetypes. They might appear as a warrior, a healer, a peacemaker, or any other symbolic figure you can imagine. We may or may not be able to identify them concretely, or perhaps they show up as a spiritual being such as a mystic, monk, priestess, or even a figure such as Jesus, Mary, or the Buddha.

Finally, we have ancestors of the heart or the spirit ancestors. These are the people we have connected to throughout our life who may not be related to us by blood or marriage but consider us family nonetheless—the high priestess who taught you everything you know, your best friend's mom who made you brownies every weekend at sleepovers, or that elderly neighbor you've sort of adopted as your own because he's lonely and kind and sings delightfully bawdy sea shanties.

Keep in mind that for genealogical and linguistic purposes, an ancestor is someone from whom you're directly descended—your parents, grandparents, and so on. Family members who can call *you* an ancestor—children and grandchildren—are your descendants. If you've suffered the tragedy of losing a child or grandchild, you can certainly work with them and speak to them as one of your beloved dead on your altar even though they are not technically an ancestor. After all, the rest of your kinfolk are probably watching over them, keeping them safe, and guiding them in the realm of those who have passed on until you join them yourself someday.

In many cultures around the globe, ancestors are venerated and honored. But for those of us in the Western world, somewhere along the way, we become so immersed in doing really important things that we stopped paying attention to the voices of our ancestors. It's not that they aren't talking to us ... we're just not paying attention.

Every single one of us has badass ancestral guides who are just screaming to be heard. Once you open yourself up to actually *listening* to them, you can form a relationship that will allow you to work with them both as a group and one on one.

Hold on a minute ... *work with* them? You're probably wondering if that's a typo—shouldn't it maybe be *worship*? Well, no. The word *worship* has some very distinct implications, and while you're certainly welcome to worship any of your ancestors you want, try thinking of it more in terms of working in tandem with them. Despite whatever spiritual path you may have grown up with, ancestral guides typically don't expect you to follow them, but to walk *beside* them. Again, it's about building a relationship.

To look at it another way, imagine you and I ran into each other in Starbucks, not knowing each other, and I looked at you over my iced coffee (a splash of coconut milk, two pumps of classic, and a shot of espresso) and said, *Hi! We've never met, but I've got this thing that I really need your help with. Can you stop what you're doing and give me some money and also pay attention to me for a few weeks or months or maybe even years so I can get what I want?*

I'm guessing your answer would be no because you don't know me, and I don't know you. We don't have a relationship. You owe me nothing, and really, can you put aside all of the other things in your life to help me do all these big things with no reciprocal benefit to yourself? Frankly, I'd be worried about you if you were the sort of person who'd say yes to such an obnoxious, presumptuous request.

On the other hand, if we've already got a friendship and I tell you that I could really use your aid with something, you might just be able to offer your support in some way. You might gift me with guidance and insight, wisdom and suggestions, or perhaps even material or financial assistance, if I really needed it. If you're able to build meaningful relationships with your people, you'll find that they will be there for you when you need a badass ancestor in your life the most.

In *Badass Ancestors: Finding Your Power with Ancestral Guides*, we're going to explore how you can work with these different types of ancestors to find, develop, and ultimately celebrate the personal power of your own inner badass.

To begin, we'll explore the history of ancestor veneration around the world. Why should any of us spend our time talking and listening to those who are long since dead? What advice could they have to give us? By looking back at the history of ancestor veneration around the world in different cultures, we can incorporate our knowledge of the past into present-day actions.

Next, plan on a crash course in genealogy research. If you've never studied your family tree, ancestor work is a great catalyst for it. Get to know the people whose blood runs through your veins and their history. Awareness of your ancestors' stories will help you connect with them on a much deeper level than just a collection of names and dates. This will also include some tips on honoring ancestral guides if you are adopted or have voluntarily chosen to sever family ties.

You'll learn how to uncover those ancestral guides. Where are they? What do they want? It's time to work with them on an individual and collective basis, so we'll discuss some daily meditations and personal power mantras that you can use to build self-confidence, empowerment, and overall badassery with your ancestors' assistance.

We'll also talk about how to work directly with your kinfolk. After all, they have their own unique set of needs and wants. What do they demand from us? What is the best way to honor them? Should we just offer some milk and cookies and call it a day, or is there more involved when calling upon our badass ancestors? What should you be asking them for? This section will address the key takeaways of working with familial spirits, archetypes, and heart ancestors in a respectful and mutually beneficial manner.

Of course, we'll also have a discussion about the problem ancestors mentioned earlier, because let's face it: some of us come from stock that we're not exactly thrilled about. However, for better or worse, these people are still a part of your DNA, and they still have made you the person you are today.

In addition to finding and identifying your people, *Badass Ancestors* focuses on a series of rituals, meditations, and other practices that can be used to bring us closer to those who walked before us. You'll learn how to set up an ancestor shrine, make offerings, and work respectfully with your kinfolk. You'll discover ways to welcome your guides into your own life in a way that impacts your physical, emotional, and spiritual well-being. Each of these workings will include specific calls to action.

Ultimately, this is a book designed for anyone who's ready to embrace their personal power and wishes to feel a deeper, stronger sense of connection to their heritage, their family, and their spiritual world. It's for anyone who's ever looked at the people in their family tree and thought, *Wow, she was a badass … I wish I could be more like her.*

It's my hope that by working with the ancestors using the ideas in this book, you'll find the empowerment, strength, and badassery that you've been looking for.

Chances are you've had it all along.

One
ANCESTOR VENERATION AROUND THE WORLD

Even though many people today are embracing the concept of ancestor work, it's hardly a new idea. Nearly every ancient culture venerated those who came before them, in some way, shape, or form, and it's not uncommon at all to look back through history and find ways that people celebrated their badass kin.

From an anthropological standpoint, the veneration of the ancestors is considered one of the earliest forms of spiritual or religious expression. There is some question as to what actually constitutes ancestor worship in early societies, and a number of variables. Some societies honored collective ancestors rather than linear ones, and there are different ways, across cultures, that the living can be influenced by the dead.

In a 2016 study, *Hunter-Gatherers and the Origins of Religion*, researchers Hervey C. Peoples, Pavel Duda, and Frank W. Marlowe proposed that there's a direct correlation between ancestor veneration and the appearance of shamanism. In early cultures that practiced ancestor worship, in one form or the other, the existence of shamanism almost always appears to indicate a stable society. In groups that don't practice shamanism but do venerate their dead, society appears a little shakier economically, politically, and

culturally. In addition, many of the groups that still practice ancestor veneration today, as their forebears did, believe that the dead
have a profound and powerful influence over the living.

The Early Period

Scholars have spent a lot of time evaluating, from an anthropological and archaeological perspective, the funerary practices of
the ancient Middle East, particularly the areas that are now known
as Iraq and Syria. During the days of Gilgamesh and Hammurabi,
dead ancestors survived socially; belief in their existence after
death created a parallel world in which they wandered about side
by side with their living descendants. For the people of this region,
which the Greeks called Mesopotamia, the dead were simply a part
of daily life.

The Mesopotamians cared for their departed family members
by offering daily gifts of bread and water, as well as gathering regularly to honor the cult of their ancestors. They wrote epic poems
and songs and prayers honoring their dead. In their work *In Remembrance of Me: Feasting with the Dead in the Ancient Middle East,* Virginia Rimmer Herrmann and J. David Schloen tell the story of a
man named Katumuwa, who commissioned a stone monument to
be carved with his image and his name, along with instructions for
his descendants to honor him annually with a great feast. His monument was uncovered in 2008; his memorial—officially known as
the Katumuwa Stele—is one of many found in Turkey and other
parts of the Middle East. Katumuwa's inscriptions shed light on
the practices of his people, particularly because the text explains
that his soul itself is present in the stone to receive the offerings
of his children and grandchildren for generations to come. How
badass would it have been if your great-something grandparents, a

century or two ago, had left you a To Do list with guidelines as to how they wanted to be honored in the afterlife?

In addition to ancestral memorials kept in private homes, there is evidence that the people of Mesopotamia also held regular banquets at tombs. Neighborhood burial areas were designated for individuals who might have held positions of prominence in the community or who were communal ancestors, and they were honored with offerings of food and drink, flowers, and incense.

The Roman Parentalia

In ancient Rome, the Parentalia was an annual nine-day celebration held each February to honor the spirits of the ancestors. All business and court activities ceased, temples were closed, and no marriage ceremonies took place. Public opening ceremonies were held on the Ides of the month, February 13, in which deified family members were welcomed with a ritual led by one of the priestesses of Vesta. A goddess of family life, the hearth, and domesticity, Vesta was worshiped in Rome for many years, and her priestesses were known as the Vestals. Don't let the idea of the Vestal Virgin fool you—the Vestals were pretty badass, and their role of tending the sacred fire of Rome was crucial to the city's security and livelihood.

Every Roman household had a shrine to the *Lares*, or spirits of dead ancestors, and the *Parentes,* who were immediate family members that had passed away, like a mother or father. When someone died, a mask was made of the person's face, and hung in the home in a place of honor. Offerings were made, both at the masks and at the tomb. The ancestors spoke through the voices of oracles when people had a question that needed answering.

Some Romans had small statuettes of their lost loved ones that they took with them if they traveled. In the film *Gladiator,* Russell

Crowe's titular character, a warrior named Maximus, prays to small icons of his dead wife and son. Maximus also invokes "blessed father" and "blessed mother," calling upon his own deceased parents in his prayers.

During the Parentalia, families gathered together to visit the graves of their deceased loved ones outside the city to avoid polluting the living. To celebrate your bloodline as the Romans did during Parentalia, visit the graves of your ancestors, and pour a libation of wine at the headstone.

Eternal Life for the Dead in Egypt

In ancient Egypt, it was much the same as in Rome—the dead were buried with great honor, pomp, and circumstance, and then sent off with all of the things they'd need in the afterlife. People actually *cared* about their dead. They venerated them long after they passed away, and celebrated them. During the New Kingdom period, around 1550–1069 B.C.E., an ancestor cult thrived in Egypt; excavations have revealed carved busts of ancestors kept in a place of honor in family homes.

In December 2018, archaeologists uncovered an 18th Dynasty villa near the site of an ancient city, Tell Edfu, several hundred miles south of Cairo. Led by professor Nadine Moeller, researchers from the Oriental Institute at the University of Chicago discovered that the villa's main hall included a shrine dedicated to the family's deceased kinfolk. The shrine contained a small fireplace and altar, numerous inscribed stelae, and statuettes of people, including a seated scribe. One of the stelae featured images of a man and woman standing beside one another surrounded by hieroglyphs that displayed not only their names and titles but also the recipe for a common offering formula.

Burial excavations from around Egypt have revealed the existence of hundreds of clay and metal pots and jars that held food and drink. This practice of sealing meal offerings along with the body into tombs is evident in the burial chamber of the man who could be considered Egypt's most famous mummified ruler, Tutankhamun, but they have also been found in the graves of average citizens. If sitting down to dine with family in life is considered a way of strengthening connections, then sharing meals with them in the afterlife is a way to keep that bond as they move onto the next world.

For those who walked the realm of the living, caring for the dead was a condition of one's status; if you treated your dead with reverence and respect, they would bless you with abundance and fortune. It was a reciprocal relationship; the dead depended on the living for a high-quality existence in the afterlife.

Mexico and Mesoamerica

In Mexico and in many Mexican communities in the United States, *Dia de los Muertos* is observed for three days, beginning on the evening of October 31 and continuing through November 2. This is the Day of the Dead celebration, a time when families gather together, pack picnic lunches, and go to cemeteries to honor the memories of family members who have died in the past year, with special attention paid to children and infants on the first day. Altars, or *ofrendas,* include colored tissue ribbons, flowers, photos of the dead, and candles. It's also popular to include food offerings with a theme of death—sugar skulls and coffins are a common item, as are small figures made of bread.

In some of the Yucatan Peninsula's smaller villages in the state of Campeche, the Day of the Dead is called *Hanal Pixan,* a Yucatán phrase that means "feeding of the souls." Photographer George Fery has spent years in Campeche, respectfully creating images that show how residents keep the bones of their ancestors in wooden crates which are then stored in colorfully painted concrete mausoleums. Fery describes the way each box is lined with a cloth embroidered by a family member that depicts the person's image, name, and a short memorial text. When visiting tombs at Hanal Pixan, family members gently remove the bones from the box, and clean them with a soft brush while praying and speaking words of praise to the deceased. After the bones are cleaned, they're covered in a fresh cloth and returned until next year's celebration.

In the Zinacantec Mayan culture of Mesoamerica, ancestral guardians formed the cornerstone of shamanistic practice. Author Robert M. Torrance explains in *The Spiritual Quest: Transcendence in Myth, Religion, and Science* that a shaman might venture on a quest, often with as many as nineteen different steps to be taken, each involving prayers, candles, and sacrifices. Making the pilgrimage from his village to the ceremonial center down the mountainside, the shaman would stop at a series of shrines to offer prayers to his ancestor gods for healing, enlightenment, and more.

Among the Inca, deceased members of the royal family were mummified and served burnt offerings and drinks. They were also watched over by a living guardian, whose job it was to ensure the deceased had everything they needed in the afterlife. In return, they were consulted for their opinions on matters of state, an extension of the idea of the Inca king's divine rulership.

In much of the Andes, ancestor worship extended beyond royal family members to include all social classes. A sixteenth-century Quechua nobleman, Felipe Huaman Poma de Ayala, spent much of his life chronicling the impact Spanish *conquistadores* had upon the people of the Andes. He wrote that after someone died, members of the extended family washed and cared for the body, providing the deceased with the reverence appropriate to their station in society. The body might be kept in a tomb, but could also reside in a relative's home shrine, where they would be honored regularly with prayer and sacrifices. This typically took place only with lineal descendants and usually only through a few generations, but it was believed that treatment of ancestral spirits had a direct effect on one's fortune and health. Disrespect or negligence would result in financial ruin and physical ailments.

You can use these practices and customs as inspiration for your own ancestor veneration if your badass kinfolk come from Mexico or Central America. If your loved ones are buried nearby, make a day of it to stop at the cemetery to clean their headstones and leave a small token or offering in tribute.

Watchful, Protective Ancestors

In some European cultures, particularly among Scandinavian societies, ancestors were buried near the home so they could keep a watchful eye on the family. The deceased helped bring honor and fortune to the surviving members; in return, the family made offerings to the dead in a specifically ritualized format (barley or beer were popular in early Germanic tribes). Families who failed to honor their dead properly could find themselves facing misfortune or catastrophe. To honor your ancestors with a Nordic theme, make offerings of food and beverage at a gravesite. Make this a formal occasion, perhaps even reciting your lineage as far back as you can, e.g., *Hail to my ancestor, Andrew, son of James, son of Ingrid, daughter of Mary*, and so on.

Among Norse societies, one of the most important gifts one could receive from their ancestors was fertile land. It was also believed that one inherited *hamingja*, or good fortune, from ancestors as well as property. An ancestor who had been successful in life was assumed to continue being prosperous in death and could grant favors and fortune to their descendants. There was a reciprocal nature to this, of course—offerings to the ancestors were the best way to invite their generosity. The dead existed side by side with the living and had the ability to bestow protection, inspiration, and power upon those who treated them well.

Eastern Spirituality

In many Asian cultures, ancestor veneration is practiced as a matter of routine. It's not so much a sense of worship as it is reverence for those who came before. This is due in part to an emphasis on family lines, and Confucius himself taught that the elders should be treated with honor. The notion of "family" was not just the people who lived in your immediate household, but your extended network of aunts and uncles, cousins and kinfolk, both living and deceased.

The Shinto practices of Japan and Buddhist practices of most of Asia include practices of filial piety; when an individual died, elaborate ceremonies would be held at both the funeral location and within the home. Just because someone passed on did not mean they would no longer be remembered, and most homes even today have a small shrine or altar dedicated to the ancestors. Offerings of fruit, incense, and flowers are presented and there is often a small tablet inscribed with the names of the deceased family members. These altars allow families to not only have a focal point for veneration of their dead but to have something to show outsiders, as a source of pride in their ancestry as well.

The living pay tribute to the dead as payment of debts owed and to show gratitude for the gifts received. As for the dead, they offer the living financial abundance, prosperity, and the blessing of descendants to honor you in the afterlife in direct proportion to how much you've cared for your own people. If you have Asian ancestors, add a small shelf on your wall with a photo of the deceased, some incense, flowers, and cups for offerings.

Native American Nations

Some of the native tribes indigenous to the Americas have always honored the spirits of their ancestors. The Iroquois of the eastern portion of the United States have a rich cultural history that includes ancestral spirits who watched over the people in their day-to-day activities as well as visiting the living during their dreams. In Iroquois society, the dead are respected and honored with regular feasts. In many Native American tribal and First Nation groups, the ancestral guides are part of a collective in which all people and animals are descended from communal ancestors.

In 1896, an explorer named Walter McClintock went to Montana, where he spent the next four years living among the Blackfoot people. In 1910, he wrote a book, *The Old North Trail*, about his experiences with Blackfoot folklore and religious customs. He relays a number of ghost stories in his narrative, including several that indicate the Blackfoot took very good care of their deceased ancestors. In some cases, they would keep the skeleton of a beloved family member in a rawhide bag for many years—one chief transported his dead brother this way for hundreds of miles, which was considered an act of great honor and devotion.

Evidence of ancestor veneration has also been found in archaeological discoveries in the American southwest among the Sonoran

Desert peoples. In *The Oxford Handbook of North American Archaeology*, Lisa Young describes shrines that include small figurines that have been found in excavations of both public areas and private households. In the same book, author Barbara Mills writes of an Anasazi site in New Mexico, where family members were memorialized with a variety of objects placed inside crypts, including adding the bones of those newly deceased to blend in with the old.

The Spirits of Africa

African Americans both in African Traditional Religions (ATR) and in mainstream Abrahamic faith systems have historically placed a lot of emphasis on the celebration and honoring of their kinfolk both living and dead. Think about it: you live in a place where you celebrate your elders and your ancestors, and then you're ripped from your homeland and sold across the sea. You have nothing at all—except your heritage. Why *wouldn't* you keep it alive, passing the customs and traditions and legacy on down for generation upon generation?

The family unit—both immediate and extended—has been the foundation of the African American community for centuries. Although the experience of the institution of slavery served to weaken the family structure in most cases—often by violent means and forced separations— it had the opposite effect collectively; it was the structure of the extended family unit that enabled survival during enslavement, through the post-Civil War era, and into the days of Jim Crow laws. As the Civil Rights Movement of the 1960s gained momentum, people spread out more, moving away from the homes where they'd been born and raised, and large family gatherings became less crucial for survival.

In *African American Elders, Cultural Traditions, and the Family Reunion,* author Renee McCoy explains the ways that African American family reunions in recent decades—often with hundreds of participants joining in from around the world—have become a vehicle for restoring lost connections and revitalizing culture and tradition. At any family reunion, itself a ritual of sorts, elders become indispensable sources of wisdom, guidance, and power; they're treated with great respect and honor, just like their ancestors. They tell stories, offer advice, and form the foundation for building strong and authentic future generations, preserving their birthright for those yet to come.

As in other places around the world, the people of different African nations and cultures honor their ancestors alongside spirits of land and place in addition to divine figures. It is the ancestors, however, who hold a special place in the spiritual system. For the Yoruba of Nigeria, not just anyone can become a venerated ancestor. To achieve this sort of status, one must have lived a benevolent life, die well-respected, and leave behind children who appropriately honor them in death by way of prayer and offerings. Sometimes, whole generations pass before someone is afforded the standing of honored ancestor.

The Kingdom of Dahomey (within present-day Benin) existed for about three hundred years and ended in the late nineteenth century when the French empire waged war and colonized the country. For the Dahomey people, ancestral rituals tied the kinship of the royal line into the fertility of the earth—crucial for a good crop and good harvest. At annual feasts, human offerings were presented to royal ancestors to bring about abundance in the fields. The ancestral spirits of the king could bestow gifts and favors upon the living if they chose; the best way to win their approval was with sacrifice. An entire ritual structure existed that celebrated the ancestors of the royal family; when a king died, hundreds of prisoners and slaves were ceremonially sacrificed so he could join his ancestors in watching over the people.

Today, people who follow many of the ATR belief systems in the West continue the veneration of their bloodlines. These ancestors maintain a spiritual connection with their living descendants; showing them honor is a way of demonstrating respect to one's elders. In general, ancestors are seen as benevolent; those who are unhappy might decide to cause inconveniences or minor problems for descendants who have wandered in the wrong direction. To appease disgruntled badass ancestors, make the appropriate offerings and ask what they want from you.

So, Where Did Our Badass Kinfolk Go?

As more and more people came to America whether by force or by choice, they brought their ancestors with them and honored them … until they didn't. What happened? Simply, we stopped paying attention to ancestral heritage. We got busy: we started focusing on having all the things our neighbors did and worrying about whether we were enough. Even though our ancestors were talking to us, we quit listening.

For many people in the Western world who were raised as Christians, the concept of ancestor worship or veneration is sometimes considered supernatural. Because it goes against scripture, people stopped doing it a few generations back; the notion emerged that ancestor worship was wrong because it goes against biblical warnings about replacing Jesus as the divine mediator between man and God.

Today, we're starting to see a resurgence of ancestor veneration as part of spiritual practice. As more and more of us embrace Pagan and nature-based belief systems, the idea that ancestor worship is somehow wrong or strange or weird is getting pushed aside. Instead, we're reclaiming our kinship lines and celebrating our ancestral guides. We're asking them to step in and help us out with healing, protection, and wealth. In return, we're honoring them. We're presenting them with offerings, gifts made in their names, and more.

After all, if we succeed, they have something to be very proud of.

Two

FINDING YOUR BADASS KIN—GENEALOGY 101

You know your kinfolk are out there ... but beyond the names of parents and maybe a couple of grandparents, most people have no idea who their ancestors really are. How are you supposed to venerate and honor and work side by side with your people when you don't even know their names? That's where some full-contact genealogy research comes into play.

In this day and age, with the technology and resources we have available to us today, anyone with an inquisitive mind and some basic critical thinking skills can unearth the stories of their badass ancestors ... and that's a crucial thing to keep in mind: the stories. You can write down names and birthdates on a chart all day long, but until you've actually learned about the history and cultural context of the people in your family tree, you're only getting half of who they are. The more you learn about the place and time in which they existed, the richer your connection with them will become.

Be warned, though: genealogy is an addictive and time-consuming hobby. You'll find yourself up until the wee hours of the morning, your partner sleepily asking when you're coming to bed while you stare at a census record or a probate court document murmuring

I'm so close to figuring this one out ... and holy cow, honey, I just found someone new ...

Genealogy is a bit like doing a jigsaw puzzle, except after a little while you realize you don't actually have the box, so you have no idea what your puzzle will look like when it's done. And as if that wasn't terrifying enough, you'll have one clump of pieces here and another clump over there that you *know* are connected but you have yet to identify the pieces that go between those two clumps. And a little bit after that, you'll have the epiphany that your puzzle doesn't even have edges—it's just going to go on forever, spreading outward and twisting over itself like a weird genetic spiderweb with you sitting happily in the center, surrounded by endless piles of marriage certificates, family bibles, and newspaper clippings.

One of the biggest questions people have about genealogy is *How much does it cost?* While paid genealogy research sites like Ancestry.com provide a valuable service and can be an incredible resource for people searching in countries other than their own, much of the information you need to get started can be found for free. At the beginning, a library card and some creative Googling can be a great way to kick off your genealogical quest for knowledge. There's a really good chance that someone has already done the work for you and all you have to do is simply connect with them.

Whether you choose free or paid services, remember that the information you obtain is only as reliable as its sources. Be sure to document everything you find, and always include original source material, e.g., scanned photos, court documents, book citations, etc., when you have access to it. There are numerous inexpensive and even free genealogy software applications that will allow you to scan or copy documents, photos, and other items into your database, so be sure to do it religiously. Otherwise, it will become nearly impossible to fact-check later on if the need arises.

Sites like Ancestry.com, Legacy Family Tree, and MyHeritage Family Tree Builder all have free versions you can access for little to no cost, although you'll typically have to upgrade to a paid version to use all features. Be sure to check the list of genealogy resources in the back of this book for information on where to find forms and charts.

Scan photos and documents and other items and save them digitally—use cloud storage if you have it or keep these files on your hard drive (remember to make backups regularly!). Use file naming conventions that make sense such as lastname_firstname _typeofdocument_year.jpg. For instance, my scanned image of the 1881 federal census, taken in Kentucky in which I identify my great-grandfather, Christopher Columbus Basham and his rather large family, is called Basham_CC_Fam_KY_FedCensus_1881.jpg. The Buckinghamshire marriage license for William Dean and Harriet Moore is Dean_Moore_MarrLic_Bucks_1862.jpg. Whatever file naming system you use, be sure to use it consistently and logically. If you don't, then at some point you'll end up with two dozen files all called CensusRecord.jpg, and that's not going to do you any good at all.

Charts and Recordkeeping

To begin researching your people, you'll want to use what's called a basic Ahnentafel chart. I know it sounds like a weird and scary word that you'd find in the potions room at Hogwarts, but bear with me here. *Ahnentafel* is a German word that means *ancestor table*, and it provides a method for organizing direct ancestors numerically. The main person—you, in this case—is always number 1.

Your father and mother are 2 and 3, respectively. Your grandparents become 4 and 5 on your dad's side, and mom's parents are 6 and 7, and so on. While this might seem confusing, you've probably seen an Ahnentafel chart before but didn't know it—it's sometimes referred to as a *pedigree chart*. The benefit of using a sheet like this is it shows your complete, direct line of ancestry all in one place. You'll find information in the appendix on where to find blank Ahnentafel charts.

As you go further back and unearth the stories of additional generations, you can add them easily. Keep in mind that a family history project isn't something you want to rush through—this isn't about just scribbling down as many names and dates as possible, in the shortest amount of time. Instead, view it as a labor of love, because it truly should be one. After all, if you want to work with your family members on a spiritual level, you really do have to take the time to get to know them. It will become a lifelong journey.

Start by putting yourself in the number 1 position. Write down the obvious things about yourself—your name, where and when you were born—because some day, someone else might be looking at this chart, trying to figure out who you are and what you did. If you're doing this on a computer, feel free to embellish it with a photo, or a link to a database where you're keeping additional stories.

For your parents, add your father at position 2, and your mother at 3. Just like you did with your own information, include their dates and places of birth. If they're deceased, be sure to add where and when they died. If you have a pair of same-sex parents, put the older one at the top, even number, and the younger one below at the odd number. Continue and add all four of your grandparents in the same way, as well as your great-grandparents (if you have their information). Remember, if you don't know specific dates or places, you can always add them later.

Here's where things get tricky for most people. Depending on your age, and the age of your parents and grandparents when you came along, you may only know the pertinent information for a couple of generations back, and that's okay! It just means now you need to start asking questions. Start by talking to your living family members. Ask them questions about their people. Here are a few things you should keep in mind as you begin to delve deeper into your family line:

Step 1: What Do You Want to Find?

There are so many different ways to approach family history; figuring out what your focus is will help you in your research. Maybe you want to find out if it's true that you had an ancestor who sailed on the Mayflower or was hanged as a witch in Salem. Perhaps you're curious about the place your ancestors lived in before they came to America. Maybe you just want to find out your family's history throughout the ages. Start with the known—yourself and most likely your parents—and work backward into the unknown. Keep in mind that the longer you wait to get started, the fewer opportunities you will have to speak to people in older generations.

Having a target in mind will help you concentrate on a specific area of research. Maybe you want to focus only on your mother's line because her people have been in the United States since 1700 and will be easier to track down than your father's people, who came over from Poland during World War II. As you seek out that target information, you're going to find a whole lot of interconnected stuff that you didn't even know was out there; save all of it, because it will be relevant later as you continue to build your jigsaw puzzle.

Take any potential stories about your family you want to explore and figure out where you can get more information. Things like newspaper articles, military records, the National Archives, and even Wikipedia might help you with the specifics of a story. If you've heard rumors that you've got a famous (or infamous) ancestor, this can also be a great place to start, because it's not just interesting, it's entertaining and will make for some nifty dinner table conversation.

After thirty years of digging around in my family tree, I discovered a very remote and obscure connection to a gentleman named John Henry Holliday, a dentist by training, born in Georgia, died in his thirties in Colorado. This might have been yet another name in the cousin collection except that John Henry was better known by his nickname, Doc, and was famous for a gunfight at the O.K. Corral, along with his buddy, a guy named Wyatt Earp. Interestingly enough, my children's father is distantly related to Earp, so everything seems to come full circle.

If you're hoping to build a general family history, it's okay to cast a wider net than focusing on a specific person or group of people, but remember that the broader your target search, the more information you're going to have to parse through as you go. That sifting can become overwhelming, especially if you're new to ancestry research. Allow yourself the luxury of scaling back if you need to, just to avoid burnout. Also, remember that not every ancestor is going to be easy to find right off the bat. That's not a bad thing, but it can present a unique set of challenges. If you hit a wall on one branch of the family tree, you can either move forward with other ancestors or keep at it by finding creative solutions to unearthing these elusive kinfolk.

Step 2: What Information Can You Start With?

It's really tempting to start looking for distant ancestors right away, but doing so can be counterproductive. Break out the old photo albums in Granny's cedar chest—old pictures and diaries and bibles can be a gold mine for clues. Talk to your living family members. Remember that whatever you're told might not be completely accurate due to how memories and stories change over time, so also be prepared to use research to confirm what you hear. Ask questions, especially of the older folks, because they'll probably be thrilled that you're interested in what their lives were like before you came along. If they don't live nearby, mail or email them a questionnaire, with questions on it like:

- Where and when were you born? Did you have older or younger siblings?

- Where did you grow up? Do you remember the house you lived in as a child? How did your family come to live there?

- Were there other relatives that lived nearby, like your grandparents, cousins, or aunts and uncles? Did you spend a lot of time with them?

- Where did you go to elementary school and high school? Did you attend college or join the military as a young adult, or did you enter the work force? What were those experiences like?

- Did you practice a particular religion when you were growing up? How often did your family go to church, temple, or other religious events? Is it the same religion you practice now? If not, what changed for you?

- What were the most important national or world events in your lifetime? How did you feel about them when they were happening, and afterwards?

- Who is the oldest relative you remember from your childhood? What do you remember about them? Are there any family stories that we're related to someone famous?

- What is the full name of your spouse? How did you meet? Where and when did you get married?

Use your Ahnentafel chart and family group sheets (remember the Appendix has information on where to find blank charts) to figure out what you've already got. You might be surprised to find that you have much more information at your fingertips than you were aware of. As an example, I had a box of papers from my late grandmother's apartment that, when finally opened years after her death, contained not only her marriage certificate from 1935 but also her birth certificate, my grandfather's birth certificate, their original social security cards, and my grandfather's military discharge paperwork. It was a treasure trove of places and dates, right there in my own desk drawer, and it allowed me to create a more complete picture of their lives, their marriage, and my grandfather's military service.

Step 3: Start the Research.

This is my favorite part because I'm a history major who also happens to be an information junkie. As you move from the known to the unknown, build the information on each person. Consider things that are more important than just the name—as an example, one of the English branches of my family tree had an unfortunate habit of naming everyone either William, George, or John. I have *seven* men whose information I have unearthed, born within one decade and five miles of each other, all named William Dean. At least two of them married women named Harriet, and two more married women named Elizabeth. Learning about them individually helps me keep them straight: there was William the blacksmith, William the farrier, William the carter, and so on.

Use other facts to figure out whether you're looking at the right or wrong person in the records, because if something doesn't match up, you could end up on the wrong branch of the tree ... or even someone else's altogether! I was trying to find an obscure birth certificate for a person with a fairly uncommon name. I finally found what I *thought* might be the right one, because the name, location, birth month, and day were correct ... but he would have been five years younger than the ancestor I was looking for. This wasn't necessarily a problem, because mistakes can and are made (I've found people whose birth years were simply written down incorrectly on official documents) but then I found him on a census record. Under the "Race" column, he was listed as Black, as were his parents. Since the man I was hunting was most definitely not a person of color, I knew this couldn't be the correct person, even though I really wanted him to be. I eliminated this guy from my search and eventually found the right birth certificate ... for a white guy, in the right year.

If you're in doubt about whether or not the person you've found is really the correct one, try going forward in time to narrow things down. If you know Captain Wentworth married Anne Elliot in 1821 but you find a record for him marrying Louisa Musgrove in 1820, you've probably got the wrong man—find the correct Captain Wentworth, because he's out there.

Census records are a great way to figure out if you're looking at the right person because you can see who's associated with them.

Entire households are listed together. If your person shows up with a bunch of names that aren't the ones you're familiar with, it may not be the right individual at all, so you'll need to explore further. In addition, you can also use census records to figure out who lived next door or on the same street. A significant pile of my ancestors all lived in the same census district in western Kentucky, and I can track their migration from one decade to the next simply because their households are listed on adjacent pages all over the area surrounding the town of Hawesville.

Some people find that creating an actual timeline is one of the best ways to keep track of which ancestors they're hunting for. Are you stuck on someone who was born in the nineteenth century but can't track down their birth certificate? That's okay. Begin with their date of death, add in the year they got married, and work your way backwards. It's possible that the birth information will turn up later, or at the very least, you can work with an approximate year in which they were born.

Keep in mind that particularly with older records, you might find variations on someone's date of birth, so allow yourself the flexibility of a year or two (or even more) in either direction. People lie about their ages all the time, and record-takers sometimes get things wrong not for any nefarious reasons but simply because human beings make mistakes. Some of my great grandmother's information says she was born in 1892 and other things say she was born a year earlier. Which is right? Who knows … but I know that if I find information on someone with her unique name in either of those years, it's worth exploring. Look at the big picture when comparing facts rather than just homing in on a single one.

Get Organized

You'll need a way to keep track of everything you find—photos, records, et cetera. If you're using a genealogy software program, they can generate forms like pedigree charts and family group sheets. Online databases like Ancestry and Family Search allow you to create your records in their system. If you want a program that can be used offline as well as when you're using the internet, consider Family Tree Maker, which will sync to Ancestry if you tell it to.

If you're not someone who likes to use digital databases, that's okay, although it does mean your work will be a little bit more labor-intensive. You can create folders, notebooks, shoeboxes—you name it—but the key is to develop a logical system. Keep your Smith ancestors in one binder and the Jones family in another. Create separate sections for various branches of the family as well as a place where you can store copies of important primary documents, photos, and more.

No matter how you choose to organize your information, it's important to be consistent, and stay organized from the very beginning, if you don't want to find yourself bogged down in piles and piles of documents with no rhyme or reason. There's no one right (or wrong) way to keep your family history work organized, but ideally the best method is the one that works for you personally. Here are a few things to keep in mind when you're organizing your ancestors, whether it's digitally, on paper, or a combination of the two.

- Decide exactly what you need to keep organized. Is it primary sources, like birth and death certificates, marriage licenses, and census records? Are you also going to include information found on websites; pages photocopied from history books; and images of people, places, and events?

- Do you want to organize by surname, by family group, or by location? Will it be easier to keep your English and Irish people in one place, for example, with your South American ancestors in another folder or filing box?

- In addition to keeping digital records of items you've scanned, you'll need a place to safely keep original copies of older documents. A birth certificate from the turn of the century or a newspaper clipping from the 1800s is not going to last long if you toss it in a shoebox. Consider investing in archival quality sheet protectors so those papers are still legible in the future.

- If you're someone who loves folders and filing, consider using a color-coded system. Use blue for your paternal grandfather's ancestors, green for your paternal grandmother's, red for the ancestors of your maternal grandfather, and wrap it up with yellow for anyone related to your maternal grandmother.

- If you're tech-savvy, consider adding metadata to your digital images, either via a graphics editing software or through special photo labeling programs. Metadata is descriptive information embedded into the digital file itself which is great because it stays attached to the image. If you move it to another computer, share it by email, or post it online, that data will always be there, so anyone who opens that photo will know it's a photo of Cousin Johan and Aunt Rumi on their visit to a Parisian café back in the 1950s.

Keeping organized from the very beginning is going to pay off in the long run. Remember, genealogy research is a marathon, not a sprint. If you want to get to know your ancestors, this is going to be a lifelong project, so take the time to do it efficiently from the start.

Types of Records

There are billions of records out there to be explored, depending on who you're looking for and what you're trying to find out. Many are available and free to the public, although you may have to do some creative digging to locate places of residence. Nearly all records will fall into one of these categories:

The United States Census

The federal census has been taken every ten years since 1790, and most of the records still exist today; unfortunately, most of the 1890 census was lost in a fire. Because there is a 72-year limit on access to census records thanks to privacy concerns, as of 2020, the most recent census you can access is from 1940. Don't worry, though; you'll be able to get your hands on more eventually, because the 1950 census will be released to the public in 2022, and the 1960 one in 2032.

The National Archives has the federal census on microfilm available from 1790 to 1940, and most have now been digitized and are viewable online via websites like Ancestry.com and Family Search.org. The best way to work with census records is to start with the most recent one and work backward. If you find someone listed in a census for a particular year, don't stop there! You can figure out numerous family relationships by checking other census records in either direction. Following census trails, you can figure out who moved out, who was born, who probably died, who moved back in, and who got married.

For census records prior to 1850, sometimes the information is a bit sparse; it may only include the name of the head of household—which is pretty much always going to be a white male—and the number of other people living in the home. In some states, that number will be broken down by race, as well as free or enslaved status, and includes gender and age groups of residents, for free whites, free people of color, and enslaved persons. From 1850 onwards, the federal census included information on every single person in the household, including their name and race, how old they were when the census was taken, and where they and their parents were born. It also includes how they were related to the head of the household, their occupation, and sometimes whether they could read or write English.

While the National Archives lacks the resources to do census records searches on your behalf, you can find this information at the regional National Archives locations in a dozen U.S. cities, as well as on numerous websites. You can also check with your state archives and your local public library to see what databases they have available to patrons as part of their access.

Census records exist in other countries as well and can be a wealth of information that takes you down the rabbit hole of making family connections. As an example, in an 1861 census record in High Wycombe, Buckinghamshire, Elizabeth Ruggins Dean lives with two of her four adult children—her husband had run off and left her some twenty years before. In 1871, someone else appears in the household, a 35-year old man named Edward Ruggins, who is listed as Elizabeth's nephew. Traveling two decades backwards to 1851, in the same town, and on the same street, fifteen-year-old Edward appears with his parents, John and Sarah Ruggins. With this information, I was able to discover that Elizabeth was not only the sister of John Ruggins, but also the daughter of Joseph Ruggins and his wife Fanny, and the granddaughter of Charles Reynolds. If I hadn't stumbled upon adult Edward in 1871, I'd have never connected Elizabeth to her parents and grandfather.

If you study enough census records, you may start noticing patterns that clue you in to the history of industry in a region, which is all part of constructing the story of your people. A significant chunk of my family hails from the aforementioned High Wycombe, and during the nineteenth century, it was a production center for the wooden Windsor chairs—today, there's even a High Wycombe Chair Museum! But even if I didn't know this already, I'd have been able to figure it out by the occupations listed for many people in the town. It wasn't just my ancestors, but their neighbors too worked as benchmen, bodgers, and framers, oh my!

Birth Certificates and Baptismal Records

A birth certificate can tell you not only when someone was born but where, and give important details about the child's parents, often including when and where they were born, too. Be sure to always use birth names in your genealogy research. That means that if Mary Miller grew up to marry John Jackson, don't list her as Mary Jackson. Keep her as Mary Miller in your recordkeeping. Birth certificates are state issued documents, so they can contain very different levels of information. My birth certificate from one state doesn't show my parents' names at all: I'll have to order the long-form record from the Vital Records department if I need that information, but my children's paperwork from the next state over includes both me and their father.

One of the issues with birth certificates is that they're harder to obtain than death or marriage records, again, because of privacy issues. I don't want you to be able to get a copy of my birth certificate—and you likely don't want me having yours—until long after I'm dead. Typically, you'll run into roadblocks obtaining birth records issued in the past hundred years. Most US states have a time period of several decades after the birth before anyone can obtain those records, and some states even have a waiting period after the person is dead. Some places will allow you to order non-certified copies of birth certificates for genealogical research purposes. Check with the municipality where you want to order a birth certificate and proceed accordingly.

If the birth record is more than a century old, you should have no problem getting it if it exists, but that's another genealogical conundrum. Most states in the US did not have a standardized record keeping system for vital records until around the end of the nineteenth century. Some places were better at recordkeeping than others; if you're looking for birth certificates in New England, for instance, you'll have more luck than someone hunting for that information in Arkansas or a rural village in eastern Montana. You might be able to find information at a county level instead, in newspaper birth announcements, or in family bibles. In many places, there was no formal registration of a child's birth, but you can instead use baptismal records from a parish registry.

Not everyone is baptized these days, but it was pretty common in the past. A baptismal record will list the date of baptism and the child's parents. It may also list the date of birth, or at least help you narrow it down through process of elimination; if someone was baptized in April 1832, you know that they could not have been born in December 1832, or in 1833. These are mostly only found in church records, and they vary widely in the information they contain, but can be great sources for names of children or other relatives, and clues about where to look for property or other records.

Death Certificates, Wills, and the
Social Security Death Index

Some genealogists recommend starting research with death certificates, for a couple of reasons. First of all, it's the most recent record, so it's going to make it easier to follow the "move backward" approach to family tree research. Remember, a death certificate is issued in the place where the person died, not where they are buried; the two are not always the same thing.

At the very least, a death record typically will include the date and place of death, the cause of death, and very often information about either the decedent's spouse and family, parents, or both. Next of kin will be listed, and typically you'll also see the name of the deceased person's father and mother, although like with birth certificates, this varies by state.

Often, you'll get lucky and the death certificate will tell you where and when the person was born. Even if it simply says the age, that will give you a target idea of where to seek out birth records. Someone who died in 1910 where the age at the time of death is listed as sixty years old was born in 1849 or 1850. Keep in mind, though, that other than the date, place, and cause of death, most of the information on a death certificate is supplied by a family member, who is often referred to on paper as the informant. If the informant was certain her father was born in Missouri and was sixty years old when he died, but he was really only fifty-eight and was born in Illinois, that can throw off your search. Consider that when you're following up on additional leads based on death certificate information.

Although today many people have a will, in the past, it was something our ancestors often did only if they had property to leave behind. Those who had nothing, or who were illiterate, typically didn't leave wills. However, if you're lucky enough to find a will from an ancestor, you can learn things like the names of their children, spouse, or siblings. Be sure to check to see who signed as the witness for the will, or whose names are mentioned in probate—these can give you clues as to the names of other close friends or family members.

The Social Security Death Index, which is searchable online, will tell you the date of death, date of birth, when and where a person's Social Security number was issued, and the city where benefits were last paid. It is fully searchable online and easy to use. However, this only helps for those ancestors who had Social Security Numbers issued *and* who are now deceased, so it isn't much help before 1950, and is somewhat incomplete up to around 1970 or so.

Marriage Records

Public marriage records will include the date of the marriage, the age—and sometimes date of birth—of those being married, and often their parents' names. In many cultures, the place of marriage can be a great clue to find the bride's birthplace, as the wedding typically took place in her hometown. Also, in older marriage records, you may find the names of a family member of the bride or groom—an aunt or uncle, older sibling, or a cousin—signing as a witness.

When you search for marriages, it's tempting to hunt with the names of both spouses. However, in most databases, this tells the system that both names have to appear in the records for you to have a successful hit. In the event that the marriage record was indexed incorrectly, it might never appear in your search results. For instance, my 2x great-grandmother was named Susan Tinnell on her marriage certificate ... but on census records, living with her parents, she was Susan Tindle. When I searched for her marriage to Christopher Columbus Basham, Susan Tinnell never appeared, and it looked as though the marriage hadn't taken place. To bypass this issue, search by one spouse at a time. Once I hunted for Christopher Columbus Basham by himself, his marriage information popped up. As a bonus, you might find that your ancestor was married more times than you were aware of! Be aware that if a woman was marrying for the second time, she'll be indexed not under her maiden name, but under her married name from the first time around.

Also remember that in years gone by, people often used their nicknames on their legal paperwork. William becomes Bill, Albert is Al or even Bertie, Elizabeth turns into Eliza or Betsy or Bess, and Mary is Molly, Polly, or something completely different. That marriage between Jonathan and Margaret could be listed as *Jon and Peggy*. Not only that, Jonathan could be listed as *Jn*, because abbreviations were popular and commonly used in the past. Jonathan's brother William may not be Bill but *Wm*, and their cousin George is *Geo*. And their sister Margaret? Forget Meg or Peggy—she's now listed as *Mag^t* and Aunt Elizabeth is *Elizth*.

Sometimes you'll run into a case where there's just no documented marriage record at all, because your ancestors got married some place that didn't require it to be formalized with the court. Other times, as I encountered in Hanover County, Virginia, the courthouse where records were kept was destroyed by a fire. Under these circumstances, you can look for alternative information, like the posting of banns—this was a tradition in England, colonial America, and several European nations announcing a couple's plan to marry on a certain date, and typically had to be repeated two or three times before the marriage could take place. If you're doing your genealogy work in middle-period Europe, check parish registers for notes of marriage services. Look for marriage announcements in newspapers as well—you might not have your great-something grandparents' marriage license, but that lovely write up in the city newspaper's Style section will provide lots of juicy information.

Passenger Lists and Naturalization Records

Immigration records, whether they come from a ship's manifest or a naturalization record, are useful, because if your ancestors emigrated to the United States, they had to get there somehow, and for most of history, that meant a ship. Passenger lists usually enumerate every single passenger, so they are good for linking spouses and children; they often include ages, too, as well as port of origin. Entire families are listed together, which can be incredibly valuable. The passenger list of the ship *Susan and Ellin*, which sailed into the Plymouth Colony in Massachusetts in 1635, shows me that not only was Joanna Pynder—or Pinder, depending on which source I'm looking at—just fourteen when she left her home in England, but also that she traveled with her mother Mary, as well as four of her sisters, all of whom are listed by name, along with their ages. I can also tell that Joanna's father Henry and her two brothers *didn't* sail on the *Susan and Ellin*, so they must have come to Plymouth on some other ship at another time.

Many colonial ship records are available online, as well as in historical societies and the National Archives. If your people voluntarily came to the United States between 1855 and 1890, Castle Garden was the first official immigration center in America, and you can search their online database for the records of over ten million immigrants that arrived from 1830 to 1892. After Castle Garden, Ellis Island became New York's processing center for new arrivals, and more than 20 million immigrants passed through the gates between 1892 and 1924; nearly all of their records are searchable online and often include photographs and digital images of documentation.

Naturalization is the process by which an immigrant becomes a legal American citizen, so these records can provide a researcher with information such as an ancestor's date and place of birth, their occupation if they had one, the year they came to the United States and how and when they arrived, and information about their home country. If your ancestor emigrated before 1906, any court—municipal, county, state, or federal—was permitted to grant citizenship, so you'll need to contact the state archives where the naturalization took place, in order to search county and local court records. These state and local records are not typically available through the National Archives. Records for naturalizations that took place after 1906 are maintained by the Immigration and Naturalization Service (INS) and are generally only available to view at a National Archives location.

Also prior to 1906, federal law extended American citizenship to the wife and minor children of any male naturalized immigrant. This means that once the head of the household was naturalized, so was the rest of the family; unfortunately for those of us who like to do research, it was not required that the wife or children were named in the records.

Draft Cards

Today any young man who turns eighteen has to register for the Selective Service. In the past, they filled out draft cards, which come in handy for finding men who would have been the right age for military service. Several drafts have taken place in U.S. history, and even if your ancestor never served in the military as an active duty member, he might have had to fill out a draft card.

These can give you name, date, and place of birth, place of residence, and even sometimes a physical description. For many, there is also a box that includes the name of a person who will always know how to find the individual's whereabouts. This is typically the wife, a parent, or a close sibling.

Another great feature of the draft cards issued during the two World Wars is that of occupation and employer. By looking at a pair of draft cards from World War I, I was able to piece together that my great-grandmother's first husband had, after abandoning her and their baby, gone off to Kansas City, where he lived with and worked for his sister's husband as an electrician before moving to Arizona, where he eventually ended up in a transient camp before dying in a hospital.

Information on the draft cards was supplied by each registrant personally but then written down by a registrar. While there was certainly a chance that there might be a spelling error or transposed letters, each person had to sign his card to attest that the information was recorded accurately, so the margin of error is fairly insignificant.

Family Bibles

A family bible can be a treasure trove of info if you can find one; in many cases, the record of someone's birth, marriage, or death, only exists because someone wrote it in a bible. For a good part of history, at least in the years before vital records registration was mandatory nationwide, family bibles were used to document the more significant events in the history of a family. They were also used in many cases by families that needed to prove when—and even if—these events took place, for legal matters like determining an heir, securing benefits for military pensions, or even enrolling a child in school. By the early part of the twentieth century, the family bible—often a prized possession and a valued gift to newlywed couples—was becoming obsolete.

If you're lucky enough to have come into the possession of a family bible, it's a great starting point for information! But like every other aspect of family tree research, consider your sources, and evaluate how reliable they are. Because information was often added years after an event took place, it's possible that some dates are inaccurate. Be sure to check the bible's publication date; any births, deaths, or marriage that took place prior to it but are still written down could be suspect. At the very least, you'll want to find corroborating evidence elsewhere.

If you didn't inherit the family bible, don't sweat it—neither did most of the rest of us. However, if you know there's one out there somewhere and you just haven't been able to locate it, reach out to relatives first. It's entirely possible that your third cousin Ardelle has it sitting on a shelf in her family room surrounded by her Precious Moments figurines. If nobody has it but everyone swears it exists, check online auction sites and used book dealers; family bibles come to them via estate sales all the time.

You can also search online for people who have taken the time to transcribe family bibles in their possession. The Daughters of the American Revolution (DAR) website has an online index of more than 80,000 family bible records, all fully searchable. The Library of Virginia has several thousand bibles in their repository, many of which can be searched for records of families in that state.

Obituaries

When I was a kid, I loved reading the obituaries in the newspaper. These very public death announcements are awesome because they will nearly always list the names of the survivors—that means the spouse and kids and grandkids—and sometimes the names of the parents and siblings. You can also use it to identify close family members who may have predeceased the person in the obituary.

Keep in mind that like many other documents, an obituary is written by the survivors of the deceased, so while you can hope that they're accurate in their recollections, it's also important to consider this a secondary source rather than a primary one. After all, you don't know who wrote it! Again, it will provide some good hints for where to look next for original documentation. I had an ancestor who had sort of disappeared from the records for several decades, and for thirty years, I was unable to find his death record, even though he's most definitely dead by now. However, by reading his sister's obituary, I was able to identify the state in which this missing ancestor lived in his later years, and that helped me redirect my search to the Southwest, where I finally found his death certificate.

Where do you find an obituary? The most obvious spot would be the hometown in which your ancestor lived, but that might not always be the right answer. Relatives in other towns may have published the obituary in their local paper as survivors. Perhaps the deceased lived in Tampa but spent his formative years active in the community in Chicago—it wouldn't be unreasonable to post a death notice in a Chicago paper. Maybe a paper in a small suburb was chosen over a larger metropolitan newspaper because of price constraints—some papers charge a fee to print a death notice, others don't. If the deceased was older and had moved in with caretakers in a new town, the obituary might be in the local paper, rather than the place where the person spent the bulk of their life.

To find an ancestor's obituary, keep your search broad and then narrow the field—this will help you avoid missing clues that are hidden in strange places. In addition to searching with the word *obituary*, also use *death notice, funeral, in memoriam,* or *memorial.* If you know that the person died of something other than natural causes, you may be able to find newspaper articles that aren't obituaries but still contain leads to follow later. I've never found a formal obituary for the mother and her four children that died on the same day in 1883 in Kansas ... but I did find a newspaper article detailing the horrific fire that killed all five of them. It included the date of their deaths, the names of the surviving family members who escaped the blaze, and far more ghastly details than I really wanted to read.

Sometimes, obituaries will give you clues as to where the person is buried as well. If funeral services are included as part of the notice, you'll be able to determine what cemetery to look in for headstones or other memorials. They sometimes will include cause of death, although not always. Watch for key phrases like *passed away after a lengthy illness* or *died unexpectedly* for clues.

In addition to obituaries, be sure to check out crowd-sourced websites like FindAGrave.com and BillionGraves.com. These are user-generated from volunteers around the world who have taken the time to document headstones and grave records. You may even be able to find a photo of the gravestone, which is wonderful information to have in cases where you can't find an obituary for one reason or another. Once you've identified a family member on one of these sites, you may see comments and legacy notes from *other* family members whom you didn't even know existed, and you'll have found one more piece in your genealogical jigsaw puzzle.

Historical Context Clues

As you're working, uncovering all the weird little nooks and crannies as you shake out the branches of your family tree, be sure to look at the bigger historical picture of your ancestors, and ask WHY they lived where they lived. When your people came to the United States or whatever country they landed in, what was happening in the place they lived before? Was there a war, civil unrest, famine, religious persecution? Why did your ancestors settle where they did? Why did they move when they did? For example:

- Many American families relocated in the early years of the twentieth century in search of new opportunities. Often, they left economically depressed rural communities and headed to the big cities. My great-grandmother and at least two of her siblings left their holler in western Kentucky, took a train north, and settled in Chicago.

- During the years of Jim Crow, many African Americans fled the oppressive South in what came to be called the Great Northern Migration, and went north to industrial hubs like Chicago, Detroit, and Cleveland looking for employment.

- The US government has issued land grants several times to encourage migration. The Homestead Act of 1862 opened up settlement in the wild frontier of the western United States. This legislation allowed any American, including freed slaves, to claim up to 160 free acres of federal land, if they lived on the land for five years and paid a nominal registration fee. By the end of the Civil War in 1865, more than fifteen thousand homestead claims had been established, by families both black and white.

- Ireland's Great Famine (1845–1852) caused a massive wave of immigration. When the country's potato crop failed and Britain's government instituted a policy of forced removal of food staples like barley, wheat, oats, mutton, beef, and eggs, more than half a million Irish immigrants entered into the United States via the port of New York alone. According to the Library of Congress, in the 110 years between 1820 and 1930, some 4.5 million Irish arrived in America, the majority of them women.

- Some twelve million individuals were taken from Africa and enslaved; according to the *Dictionary of American Slavery*, more than half a million of those ended up in the United States during the eighteenth and nineteenth centuries. If you're researching enslaved ancestors in your family tree, be sure to check out the specific list of related resources in the Appendix.

The Issue of Name Changes

In this day and age, when everyone's information is everywhere, you'd be hard pressed to change your name and get away with it. The name on your driver's license matches the one on your credit card and on your student loans and probably on your Facebook profile. But for our ancestors before us, things weren't always that cut and dried. Name changes happened a lot—whether by accident or design—so when you're hunting for missing kinfolk, it's important to keep a few things in mind about name changes.

First of all, there's a popular myth that millions of Ellis Island—and before that, Castle Garden—immigrants had their European names Anglicized by immigration officials who couldn't communicate properly with people who were Hungarian or Czechoslovakian or whatever the case may be. More than being not entirely true, this idea is hardly ever supported by historical research. Consider the process by which immigrants entered the United States during periods of mass migration.

Passenger lists were compiled at points of departure, where the immigrant purchased a ticket. This means that if you left from Hamburg, you were buying a steamship ticket in Hamburg from someone who spoke your language. If you purchased your passage in Palermo, the person who sold it to you spoke Italian, just like you. When you got on the ship at the port in your home country, your name was written in the ship's manifest—again, by someone familiar with your language.

Once you arrived at Ellis Island, your paperwork already in hand, completed back in the Old Country, you were met by an immigration inspector who had a copy of that ship's passenger list, complete with everyone's name written on it. At least one out of three immigration inspectors were foreign-born, and most spoke multiple European languages; inspectors were often assigned to their duties based on which language group they were most familiar with. It's unlikely, simply because of the types of people working at Ellis Island, that a foreign name would confuse an immigration inspector.

In the 1950s, the Immigration and Naturalization Service (INS) went through millions of records of entry into the United States during the past century because there were people trying to obtain citizenship, after decades in the country, whose identity didn't match their immigration paperwork. This was problematic, obviously, because it meant the immigrant would face issues with not only naturalization but also with access to voting or fair trials in legal matters. The INS discovered that records of entry for many people *did* contain errors … but it wasn't because no one at Ellis Island understood them or forced them to Anglicize their name. In fact, nearly all of them happened because:

- The immigrant used a fictitious name—or that of another person—when they left their home country, which could happen for a variety of reasons

- The person's name was accidentally misspelled by a clerk in their home country, possibly by someone who was unfamiliar with that particular spelling; Shepherd might be written down as Shepard, Sheppard, or even Cheppard

- They were a child recorded with the surname of a stepfather, grandfather, or uncle they traveled with, instead of their biological father

- Errors were made due to naming conventions in other countries that didn't translate correctly into American documentation

- Women were registered under their maiden names rather than their married names

- The immigrant himself altered the name or translated it into English, to make it easier to pronounce

Certainly, there are plenty of American name-change stories, and many don't involve immigrants from other countries at all. Keep in mind that the idea of everyone knowing how to read and write is a modern novelty; go back through a century or two of census records, and you'll see variations in family spellings for the same person. My tenth great-grandfather's name was spelled at least three different ways: *Basham, Bassham,* and *Bassam* ... and *two* of those three versions appeared in his last will and testament!

Build a Story for Your Badass Kin

While you work to uncover your people, don't collect just names and dates. As you learn more, collect the history of the place and time, and the stories of the people themselves. I know that Owen Coltman was born in 1867 in High Wycombe, Buckingham-shire ... big deal. That's fairly boring, right? But knowing that Owen emigrated to America in 1888 via Philadelphia on a ship called the *British King,* settled in Chicago, and then sent for his wife Elizabeth and their son George, helps to humanize Owen and bring him to life. Elizabeth and George arrived in New York City in 1889 on the White Star liner *Britannic.* Owen and his wife eventually had four more children and several grandchildren—one of whom was my great-grandfather.

I can tell you that Lady Catherine Camell was born around 1444, was married twice, and lived all the way to age sixty-five—not unimpressive for a woman of her time, but still fairly generic and bland. Or I could tell you that her first husband, a French lord, was arrested for attempting to overthrow the king, and then murdered in an insurrection just two years later. Or that Catherine soon remarried to an English knight, and became the grandmother of Sir Francis Weston, who was beheaded by King Henry VIII in 1536, following accusations that he'd been fooling around with Anne Boleyn. Suddenly, Lady Catherine just got a whole lot more interesting, didn't she?

You can easily say that your ancestors left one country and went to another, and then just be done with it and move on to the next name on your list ... or you can learn about the culture and society of their times, so you can *feel* what it must have been like. Learn how long it would take to sail from Liverpool to Boston in the winter, or how many days it would take a cart to travel from Richmond to Roanoke. Find out why the Slovakian town your people left in the 1930s has changed its name three times in the past century and a half. Listen to the narratives of formerly enslaved people and hear their words and their stories of heartbreak and desperation and hope. Read about what it was like for the Scots when the clearances came and the pipes and tartans were outlawed, and they fled the English landowners, and weren't even allowed to speak Gaelic to one another.

Do you know what your ancestors ate? What foods were available to them, in the places and times that they lived? I'm fascinated by food anthropology—I like to study the cultural context of the things we eat and why we eat them. I'm convinced that a lot of things my ancestors had for dinner were eaten because these people were just too poor to eat anything else. My great-grandmother was from western Kentucky, and her daddy—whose occupation was formally claimed as "woodsman"—probably brought home possum and raccoon and squirrel for supper, and she and her stepmother would have cooked up greens and some hominy to go with it. You can't tell me that was considered high end cuisine.

Brush up on the cooking and staple diet of your kinfolk, whether it's the maize and bright vegetables of your Mexican *abuela's* family, hearty thick stew from a European connection, or the meats and plants of an indigenous population. Learn about what your people ate and *why* they ate it, because it humanizes them. It makes them more than just names on a chart.

What did they wear? Figure out what people of their social station would have done on a daily basis. Research the politics of their era. Was there religious conflict? Did someone coming through a port city change their name to something less Polish sounding so they could fit in with their new neighbors in America? Did an epidemic of cholera sweep through a Navajo village one day and wipe out everyone but the infant who would one day become your family's matriarch?

Take the time to do the work and learn who your people really were. Get to know them and immerse yourself in their worlds. Because these are the things that bring us closer to our ancestors and help us to honor them.

When You Have an Absent Parent

Ancestor work can be emotionally challenging. If one of your still-living parents was absent from your life while you were growing up, or if you're currently estranged from them, ancestor work can feel downright exhausting at times, but you may find that this parent's people are going to get involved in your business. Here's why.

Grandmothers and other ancestors have a tendency to call things as they see them. If your parent has been uninvolved in your life, don't be surprised if that parent's grandparents or great-grandparents start taking a special interest in you. It's possible that they'll feel extra protective of you, since their son or daughter—or grandson or granddaughter—has made the choice not to be part of your life. In cases like this, the ancestors of an absent parent are often our strongest advocates. They take on a protective role in an almost apologetic way to make up for the shortcomings of the person who abandoned us.

Just like living grandmothers and grandfathers sometimes step in as surrogates and help raise kids in extended families, our dead ones often do the same thing. Some people say that our ancestors are our first line of defense, and that includes when they need to step in between you and someone else who couldn't be bothered to be part of your life. If a parent has bailed out on you at some point—or your relationship with them is so toxic that you've decided to avoid them—don't be shocked when their people come rolling in to tell you what's what. If you want to ask them to serve as a substitute for someone who's missing in your world, all you have to do is ask— odds are good that they'll be honored and they'll oblige.

Honoring Ancestors When You're Adopted

Sometimes, for a variety of reasons, you may not have any idea who your badass ancestors could have been at all. There are a variety of circumstances that can cause this to be the case, but it's most certainly going to come up if you or one of your parents are an adoptee. For some people, the notion of kinfolk is quite simple: it's blood related ancestry, and that's it, period. However, for many other people—both within the magical community and outside of it—your family is the group of people who raised you and loved you, whether you're connected to them by DNA or not. If you agree that the idea of building a family tree is to tell a story, then that story includes the people who claim you as kin whether they're related by blood, marriage, adoption, or some other connection.

In the not-so-distant past, adoption was kept secret; families didn't discuss it, and many people grew to adulthood with no idea that their parents were not biologically related to them. Now, however, there is far more open discussion about the subject, so if you were adopted as a child, you're more than likely aware of it. You may even know who your biological parents were. Regardless of whether you do or not, your ancestor work presents its own unique set of opportunities.

Yes, opportunities. Because you've got the luxury of working with twice as many ancestors as those who are not adopted. Your adoptive family *chose* you, so you get to claim them as part of your ancestry, even if they aren't related to you by blood. They picked you out and raised you, and your adoptive parents are your mom and dad. Ask any parent of an adopted child which kid they love better—their adopted one or their biological one—and you'll get the same look of confusion and disbelief that you'd get if you asked the parent of two biological kids which one is their favorite. You've grown up around them, you've seen their family photos on the wall, and you've listened to Grandma's hilarious stories about her gin-crazed youth over Thanksgiving dinner. Your family loves you, and you love them—because you're family.

You also have the option of working with the ancestors of your biological family. Now, you may not know who they were, but *they* know *you*. There are a number of different ways to do this, but it can be tricky when you're not entirely sure where your predecessors came from. The first way, and one that works for many adopted people who have chosen not to pursue their biological parents' information, is that of honoring archetypes. Now, this is still going to require a little bit of research, but it's not nearly as complex as embarking on a DNA treasure hunt.

An archetype is a symbol—and we'll cover this in a lot more detail in chapter 8. Let's say I know that I'm of Eastern European ancestry, but not much else. That's not really a lot to work with, is it? There's a whole lot of random Eastern European people I could be connected to. However, with a little digging, I discover that there are some legends among Eastern European countries that I find I really connect with. Taking it a step further, I learn about, for example, a folktale from the Carpathian Mountains about a woman who lives in the woods, protects children from hungry wolves, and brews up magical potions. Was she real? Maybe—folktales often have some basis in reality. Maybe not—but regardless, she might be a good place to start. If I think of her as an archetypal ancestor, rather than a blood ancestor, I can still pay tribute to her as a symbol of the many people whose blood could be running through my veins.

Another way of connecting on an archetypal level is to do an ancestor meditation, which is a good way to let your mind wander back in time to see if you can connect on a metaphysical level with either individuals or archetypes who resonate with you spiritually. To do this, find a quiet spot somewhere near your ancestor altar (see chapter 3).

Close your eyes and breathe deeply. Think about who you are and what you are made of, and know that everything within you is the sum of all your ancestors. From thousands of years ago, generations of people have come together over the centuries to create the person you are now. Think about your own strengths as well as your weaknesses, and remember that they came from somewhere. This is a time to honor the ancestors who formed you. Call out to them—you don't need their names—and ask them to visit you.

Address them with respect. You can say something simple like, *Grandmothers, grandfathers, all of my people, I ask that you come into my life to guide me, protect me, and aid me. Grandmothers, grandfathers, all of my people, I honor you, and welcome you to join my life.*

As you reach out to them, there's a good chance they will appear to you and present themselves either as individual people or as archetypes—the warrior, the healer, the wise woman, the spiritual guide, and so on. No matter how they appear to you, welcome them and use these images as a foundation for your ancestral work.

It's also important to note that many people—not just adoptees—can claim some sort of mixed heritage. Although you may have grown up believing you were descended from a particular ethnic or racial group, the odds are good that you're connected to others as well. Most of us can't tell by looking in a mirror who our people are … or aren't. While DNA testing like that available from Ancestry and 23AndMe might be helpful in narrowing down a region—and result in some surprise cousins—it doesn't always tell the whole story. For instance, I've got people in my family tree that came from a small town in what is now Slovakia; they've been in that little village since around the thirteenth century. However, they're not really Slovakian at all. They're ethnically German, descended from a group of people who left Germany and went east, colonized this particular area in the Košice region, and then intermarried within their own family groups. Slovakians on paper, Germans by heritage.

In addition to honoring biological and archetypal ancestors, there is also the concept of the family of the heart and soul—these are the people who love you and count you as family, either by blood, by choice, or by happy accident. They may include your best friend's mom who let you sleep over every Friday night in high school, or your spouse's dad who likes to take you fishing, or that wonderful distantly related cousin that shows up at random to just drop off novels she knows you would like. Family of the heart and soul, for many people, is as valuable as the family you're genetically connected to, and we'll discuss those in depth in chapter 7.

If you're an adoptee, or if there's some other reason you don't have a connection to your biological family, don't sweat it. There are plenty of other ways to find a spiritual kinship to ancestral guides.

Three

YOUR BADASS ANCESTOR ALTAR

If you're going to be working with your ancestors, you should give them a place of honor in your home. After all, each member of your living family has their own space, so why can't your ancestors? Your ancestor altar can be either permanent or temporary, depending on both your need and the availability of usable space. Setting up an ancestral altar is beneficial for a number of reasons.

First of all, it will allow you to have a designated area in which to do your spiritual work. This is important, because just like any other aspect of your spirituality, there is magic to be found in the routine and repetitive. The altar forms the cornerstone of ritual practice. This, in turn, gives you the opportunity to develop your relationship with each member of your extended clan you want to work with. They know where their spot is in your home, and it's theirs because you've offered it to them.

Having an altar to your kinfolk also confers a certain degree of protection upon your home, your family, and everything you own because you're giving those ancestral spirits the chance to be an active part of your life. That means they'll protect the space in which they are loved and revered and honored. Your home becomes their home, and they'll watch out for it, and everything—and everyone—contained within.

Finally, having that ancestral altar in place will allow you greater access to your peoples' wisdom, experience, and guidance. After all, if you've got an ancestor altar right there in your living room, it's ever-present, and you can talk to and work with them at a moment's notice.

Some people do ancestor work every day, some approach their altar once a week, and some work with their ancestors just whenever they feel like it. In general, you want to get into a routine; it's important to establish a consistent practice of working whether in the form of prayer, ritual, or other interactions—at your ancestor altar. This, after all, is part of relationship building. You can't have a relationship with someone you never speak to.

Where in your home you physically place your ancestral shrine depends on your personal belief system, what you're using as an altar, and the amount of space you have. There are no universal rules on altar placement, although people in many magical belief systems are uncomfortable putting ancestors in the bedroom. If you're concerned that your kinfolk might cause a problem during intimate moments, don't put them in there. Worst case scenario, you can cover your ancestor altar with a white cloth during sexy-times. Also, do *not* put it in the bathroom. That's just plain disrespectful. Put it in a place that's conveniently located so you can see it regularly—remember the adage *out of sight, out of mind*? My altar sits adjacent to my couch, and I walk past it easily a dozen times a day. If it were in that weird, out-of-the-way back corner of my basement, when would I ever use it?

Your altar can be any available flat surface. Use the top of a dresser, a coffee table, a shelf on a wall, an end table. If you've got the space available, it's nice to use an entire table for your shrine, but you're short on room—or you have to share your living quarters with people who are less than understanding about what you're up to—you can create it any place that can be left undisturbed, so that the spirits of your ancestors may gather there, and you can take time to meditate and honor them without having to move stuff around every time someone needs to use the table. My ancestor altar is the top of an IKEA cube bookshelf that I found at a garage sale, refinished, and covered with an embroidered altar cloth to represent my heritage. The key here is that your altar needs to be large enough to hold everything you wish to place upon it at any given time.

Before you get started setting up your altar, you'll want to cleanse the space—and this is important. Just as you wouldn't invite your living grandmother over to a dirty house, you don't want to bring the dead ones into a home that's a mess, either physically or spiritually. Clean the entire area from top to bottom. You can wipe down the space regularly with a damp cloth and some lemon juice, followed by anointing the four corners and center of the altar with either consecrated water or wine, blessing oil, or whatever your particular belief system requires.

In addition to cleaning the space itself and the altar table or shelf physically, metaphysical cleansing is a must. You can do this by using smudging herbs, such as cedar, sweetgrass, yerba santa, or nag champa. Some magical belief systems use sage for smudging, and while that works well to get rid of negativity, you may find that it also keeps your ancestors away. I like to use dried rosemary, because rosemary is associated with remembrance. If you'd like to ceremonially consecrate the altar space to your people, offer a simple incantation as you clean and purify it, like so:

I dedicate this space to those whose blood runs through me.
My fathers and mothers, my guides and guardians,
my kin and clan, grandmothers and grandfathers,
wise ones who walked before me,
and those whose spirits helped to shape me.

Now that you've cleaned your space, you've smudged the area, and you've got your shelf or tabletop in place. What should you include on your ancestor altar? The sky is the limit! What do you feel called to put on there? Let's look at some basics you might want to consider.

Your Altar Cloth

Start with a cloth on the top of the altar. In some magical belief systems, particularly African Traditional Religions, the ancestor cloth is almost always plain white, which represents purity and cleanliness. However, if you're not crazy about white, you can branch out and try something that's more appropriate to your family. Consider cloths and fabrics that are culturally relevant.

Think about the materials used in traditional clothing in the country or region from which your people hail. Rich sari cloth from India, the brightly colored kente of Ghana, textiles embellished with Native American beadwork, and Scottish tartan plaids are just a few examples of the beautiful fabrics you can find from around the world. If your family's background is centered in the colonial United States, think about using linsey-woolsey, cotton, or calico. I sometimes use an unfinished quilt top that my late mother-in-law hand-stitched before her death. Do your people hail from England or France? Try brocade or toile. For people who follow some Eastern religions, a red cloth is always used. In a few Celtic-based paths, it is believed that a fringe on the altar cloth helps tie your spirit to those of your ancestors. The possibilities are endless. Figure out which one—or more—best represents your family and use that as an altar cloth if you want something more interesting than plain white. You can also use plain black, if you prefer. Whatever sort of fabric you use for your altar cloth, it should be clean and should be special; if you use it as an altar cloth, don't use it for other things as well.

If you've got the time and energy, as well as a little bit of skill with a needle and thread, you might want to try your hand at embroidering an ancestor altar cloth. This can have any design on it that you like, but it should be something that's symbolic of your heritage. Many years ago, when I was about ten years into my family tree research, I hand-embroidered my family tree—or at least, those ancestors I had discovered at the time—onto a plain muslin tablecloth, measuring five by seven feet.

My name is in the center, and all of my ancestors spiderweb outwards from me, reaching ten generations in each direction, with different colored embroidery floss for each branch. It's lovely, and I still use it for many ancestor rituals and workings. Of course, I've added a few thousand people to my collection since then, but it's still a lovely reminder of the early work I did, in honor of my kinfolk, because each and every stitch brought them closer to me.

An ancestor altar cloth is something you can make easily, and you don't even need any sewing skills to make it effective. This project can be as simple or as complex as you like, depending on your time constraints, creativity, and crafting skills.

You'll need:

- A plain white or cream-colored tablecloth, or other piece of fabric
- Fabric pencil
- Embroidery floss and hoop, or fabric markers
- A genealogy of your direct ancestors

There's no hard and fast rule about how to do this—this craft is very personalized, so do what works best for you. If you're handy with a needle and thread, you can embroider the cloth, because it will definitely last longer that way. If you're not confident in your stitching abilities, you can use fine-tipped fabric markers, but keep in mind that this option may limit your ability to wash the altar cloth if it gets dirty or stained during ritual.

Start by putting yourself in the center and writing your name carefully with a lightweight fabric pencil (the markings will wash or brush off easily when you're done). Branch out to include your parents' names above you, one on each side. Using lines to connect everyone, gradually add the names of your ancestors. You can even include dates of birth and death, or place names if you have the room.

It's best to do everything in pencil first; better yet, use Post-It Notes, one for each ancestor's name—to position people around the cloth. If you know the names of lots of ancestors on one side, but only a few on the other, it can start looking lopsided pretty quickly, unless you're able to rearrange people which is why sticky notes are so great!

Once you've figured out everyone's placement, add the names in fabric pencil until you've included as many people as you like. If you're going to embroider the names, work from one side to the other, just to keep things simple—you may even want to do different branches of the family, or different generations, in alternating colors. If you opt to use fabric markers for the final work, be careful! Stitches can always be picked out, but markers are permanent.

Keep in mind that the very act of creation can be magical, and you can use the crafting of this altar cloth as a ritual in and of itself. Particularly if you're stitching, there's a very meditative aspect to the creative process. As I stitched each individual's name into my own altar cloth, I focused on the person, who they were, what their lives might have been like. I welcomed them into my home, my heart, and my life.

Photos and Portraits

You'll also want to include photos of your ancestors on your shrine or altar. A good rule of thumb is to only include images of the deceased. That means if you've got a photo of your late great-grandma Mildred with baby you in her lap, find another photo for the altar that doesn't have you in it. Ancestor altars are for the dead, not those who are still alive. In addition, if you've got problem ancestors (covered in chapter 6) who did horrible things, you may want to leave their photos off as well. Some people include photos of beloved pets on their altar, but that's entirely up to you.

What about ancestors who lived too long ago to have a photo taken? Obviously, if you're doing ancestor work with anyone who died before about the middle of the nineteenth century, you're just out of luck with photography—and that probably seems weird, given that we live in a time where selfies are pretty much a standard part of the cultural lexicon. However, long before we were Instagramming pictures of ourselves with our best friends, before our great-great-grandparents sat stiffly for a daguerreotype, people's likenesses were captured in portraiture. Do you have a painting of an ancestor or even a line drawing? Maybe your ancestor was someone famous—a queen or a philosopher or one of America's founding fathers—and there are numerous pieces of art to choose from.

Do you have a jar or urn of cremains from one of your ancestors? Use that in addition to photographs if you have it in your possession. I've got a small jar for each of my maternal grandparents, and they sit side by side on my altar. They spent sixty-odd years together in life, and I'm certainly not going to be the one to tell them they have to be apart in death. I suspect if I tried, I'd never hear the end of it.

How about soil from the graves of your people? If you're fortunate enough to know where they're buried, consider bringing home a small sample of the earth from where they're buried. If you do this, it's important to do so respectfully and in a way that doesn't disrupt the internment. A spoonful is usually sufficient and can be powerfully symbolic. Be sure to offer your thanks when you take soil from a grave; you may even want to leave an offering at the headstone as a token of your gratitude and to honor your kinfolk.

Family Heirlooms

Family heirlooms make a great addition to your altar. What things do you have in your possession that your ancestors might have touched? Do you have that sewing case that traveled across the world and came through Ellis Island? Perhaps you've got a fancy silver fork that your great-grandmother slipped into her pocket when she fled steerage and got into a lifeboat on the *Titanic*. What about great-uncle Jimmy's dog tags from Vietnam or Grandpa Yataka's pocket watch? Do you have a picture of the family home back in the Old Country? I've got my grandmother's Blue Willow china set, which I only bring out when I plan to call upon her.

Family heirlooms help establish a connection because they are tangible objects that were actually handled by your ancestors. That bowl you are holding right now was held a century and a half ago by a pioneer woman on a wagon train. The metal hammer in your garage was used by a blacksmith who eventually became your great-something grandfather. This connection is incredibly valuable; don't overlook it.

A Drink of Water ... Or Something Else

Water in a cup is offered as a symbolic drink for the ancestors in a number of spiritual traditions. In general, avoid using tap water if you can help it; if you *do* need to use tap water, be sure to consecrate and bless it prior to putting it in a cup on your ancestor altar. In some belief systems, particularly those associated with conjure or hoodoo, the water is changed on the same day each week; often, this is on Monday, but if you have a reason to use a different weekday, use it.

Maybe your ancestors wouldn't appreciate water. That's okay! What about alcohol? Half of my family originated in Scotland, so I often have a glass of whisky on my altar; I'm convinced I'm genetically predisposed to offering a glass of Glenfidditch 21-year Reserva to anyone associated with my paternal lines. If you're not a fan of whisky, consider wine or other culturally appropriate spirits. Would you prefer to not offer liquor? That's okay; coffee or tea are frequently acceptable as drinks for your people, if you know it's something they would have consumed in life.

Sometimes, you may find yourself presenting your kin with something that came from an unexpected source. I'm not a big wine drinker at all, and yet every year during the holidays, people gift me with bottles of it, so I've always got plenty on hand for guests. A couple of years back, I ended up with a really nice bottle of Hacienda Monasterio, a Spanish red wine. I had no idea what to do with it, so it sat on top of my fridge for a good long while … until the winter of 2018, when I discovered that my 22nd great-grandfather was King Ferdinand III of Castile and Leon, later canonized as Saint Ferdinand. Hacienda Monasterio comes from the Castilla y Leon region and is made from a local variation of Spain's emblematic red grape, the Tempranillo. All of a sudden, I realized I had a use for that bottle of Hacienda Monasterio after all—in the form of an offering to an ancestor who would have consumed wine made from the very same grapes. Perhaps Ferdinand's personal stock of wine even came from a vine that was the ancestors of the ones used today in Castile's wine production.

Symbols of Your Family's Origins

Add symbols of your family's heritage to your altar. I've got a dried thistle for my Scottish ancestors, a small Viking shield for my Norse heritage, and a stone from the top of a German mountain. Do you have a flag from the country your people came from? What about a musical instrument, such as a djembe from West Africa, a set of uillean pipes from Ireland, or one of Japan's biwa lutes?

Do you have artwork hanging above your altar? Consider a tapestry depicting the Italian countryside, a painting of the iconic skyline of Saint Petersburg, or a map of Kenya. Did your people come from a country with a specific design style that has become famous? Many indigenous cultures have their own unique art; Australia's aboriginal people have a distinct style that is different from the people of the Hawaiian Islands or the First Nations people of

Canada. Look into culturally relevant designs that reflect your heritage and hang something above your altar to give the space some depth.

Candles—Lots of Candles

You should plan on including candles on your ancestor altar—and there's a lot of room for different styles and needs here. In some magical traditions, white is the only color used, and unscented at that. If that works for you, have at it—but what if Granny Sue's favorite color was red, like her trademark bright lipstick she wore to the USO dances during World War II? Maybe Uncle Al used to spend all his time fishing in the Florida Keys...and you've found a candle that smells like ocean breezes, and it's pale blue? Ask yourself what your people would appreciate the most, and take it from there.

You can use different sizes of candles, although keep in mind these few guidelines. Tealights and votives are great for workings that honor many ancestors at once. Designate each candle to represent a specific ancestor. If the working is more general, you can use one or two candles to symbolize everyone you're working with, though I'd recommend breaking them into groups—maybe you'll have one to honor your maternal grandparents who came from Hungary, another for that ancestor who emigrated from El Salvador, and still a different one for the branch of your family that traveled across the United States in a covered wagon pulled by oxen.

What about larger candles? This is where you have a lot of opportunities to be creative. Jar candles are a wonderful option for doing individualized ancestor work because you can attach pictures to them. Get a few plain jar candles, use your printer and some clear adhesive label paper, and go to town printing out photos.

Stick them on the glass, and you've got instant ancestor candles that you can work with. If you're one of the people who can count actual canonized saints in your family tree, you might even be fortunate enough to find an image of your ancestors already out there for you. Among my direct line, I have Begga of Landen, Margaret of Wessex, and Arnulf of Metz, all of whom were made saints several centuries after their deaths; while I've struggled to find pre-made saint candles with any of their images, finding artwork depicting them has been a piece of cake because they're Catholic saints; I simply print and stick.

Offerings

Something else you'll want to include on your ancestor altar is offerings. So, what's an appropriate offering? Remember where we talked about getting to know your people, with some deep research? This is one of those times when that's going to come in really handy. You've got to understand your ancestors in the historical and cultural context in which they lived. Otherwise, you're going to offer them something that's inappropriate. While that doesn't necessarily mean they're going to lay down a curse upon you and all of your future generations, they're certainly going to be far less inclined to help you if you show that you can't be bothered to learn who they are.

Here's an example. Let's say you have a friend named Steve. He likes action movies with lots of explosions, hard whisky, strippers, and death metal. You've also got a friend named Emily, who enjoys French art films, fancy wine tastings, and classical music. When Steve comes over, will you break out the baroque music and a bottle of 2008 Domaine Leflaive and watch a foreign movie with subtitles? Are you going to invite Emily over to watch the newest Jason Bourne flick and listen to Slayer with you? Probably not, because you know each of these friends well enough to know what they're into—and not into—and you're going to plan the evening accordingly.

Treat your ancestors with the same level of respect. If your people came from a Scandinavian country, don't offer them a fish that is only found in the tropics. If Grandpa Joe liked his coffee strong and black every morning for eighty years, presenting him with a cup of Earl Grey tea with milk and sugar just because *you* like it isn't going to be terribly well received. You can't go wrong with homemade baked goods, so why not learn about the breads or dishes that were a favorite in your family's country of origin?

Did you stumble across a packet of pipe tobacco just like the kind your great-something grandfather inhaled? Maybe you've got an ancestor's Revolutionary War journal in which she describes how much she enjoyed making a dress from a bolt of blue silk brought through a blockade. Offer the tobacco. Offer a length of blue silk. Use your imagination, think outside the box, and honor your kinfolk with things that will please them.

Other Goodies for the Altar

There are plenty of other things you can include on your ancestor altar. What about making a shadow box with keepsakes, photos, and other mementos? You can add religious items as well, no matter what your own belief system is. I've been a Pagan all of my life and have never dabbled in Christianity … but I do have two bibles and a Book of Common Prayer on my ancestor altar because they belonged to women in my family who wrote their names in them a century ago or more.

Make a Memorial Box

Why not make a memorial box? I use mine to specifically represent the most recently deceased family member. My kin are a long-lived bunch, so the memorial box doesn't get updated too often, maybe every few years or so. To make one, get a plain wooden box from your favorite craft store, or better yet, find one at the thrift store that you can repurpose. Sand it down until smooth, and then paint or decoupage a design on it that speaks to you. Once that has dried, add a photo of the deceased to the inside as well as some keepsakes, family jewelry, and a candle or two. If you've got a copy of the obituary, the program for the memorial service, or flowers from the funeral, add those in there as well. Keep this in a place of honor on your altar.

Handcrafts and Skills

Do you have a particular skill at a handcraft that you could use to honor your people? Try doing the work at your altar to celebrate those gifts. My great-great-grandmother, Sophia Allen, was one of eleven children born to a Quaker family in Birmingham, England, and she worked as a lace maker. It's a highly skilled line of work, and she eventually lost her sight; I don't make lace, but I do crochet, and when I'm working my hook and yarn in intricate loops and twists, I often do so by my ancestor altar, imagining what it was like for Sophia to make lace by candlelight in the damp Birmingham winters. When we engage in the act of creation, whether it's knitting or carving or painting, we are embracing hundreds or even thousands of years of tradition and embodying the spirit of all of the people who came before us.

Ritual Prayer Beads

Have you ever used prayer beads? They are popular in many religious belief systems. The best-known type is the rosary, but you don't have to be a Christian to pray or use beads. Within the rosary, each bead is representative of a prayer, which is counted in a ritual format. Some forms of Judaism have used prayer beads for many years, with a bead or knot symbolizing each of the Psalms. In some Eastern belief systems, including Hinduism, Buddhism, and Shinto, the 108 beads of the mala are used to keep count while reciting chants and mantras, or to call upon the names of deities in spiritual practice.

Making and using prayer beads can be a meditative act in itself. If you've got a set of beads already made, add them to your altar. If you don't, you can make a set pretty easily.

To make a set of ancestral prayer beads, you'll need:

- Beads in different colors to symbolize each generation
- Beads that symbolize the country or region your people came from
- Additional beads to represent specific individuals of importance
- Spacer beads in color of your choice
- Beading wire or string

Start with the generational beads. If you begin with your grandparents, you'd use four beads in one color to represent their generation, eight beads in a second color to represent your great-grandparents, sixteen to symbolize your great-great-grandparents, and so on. Sort your beads and arrange them so they form a pattern that you like. Add in the beads for different countries and regions—you may want to go with a different size or style of bead so that you can remember what each of them stands for later. If you've got individual beads to represent specific people, put them in with the appropriate generation. Finally, add spacer beads to give each section some delineation. Play around with the designs, laying them out flat before you string them; try different patterns and designs and see which feels right for you.

Once you have your beads aligned the way you like them, string them on the beading wire and knot it securely. Keep your beads on your altar, and when you're calling your ancestors, you can do so by going back through each generation and reciting the names of those represented by each group of beads. You may want to get creative and do different sets of beads for different sets of ancestors; I have one set that is very specifically Celtic, using knotwork beads, triskeles and triquetras, and so forth. My other set is a little more industrial and utilitarian and symbolizes a different branch of the family altogether.

Make a Headstone Rubbing

Are your family members buried nearby, or have you had a chance to visit the cemetery in which they reside? Add a grave rubbing* to your altar space. A headstone rubbing is a wonderful and unique way of preserving the past, but there are still some precautions that you should take when making one. If a headstone is damaged or crumbling, don't do a rubbing—take a photo instead.

To make a gravestone rubbing, you'll need lightweight paper (like white butcher's paper) as well as a large, dark crayon or rubbing wax, some masking tape, and a soft-bristled brush to gently clear away any loose debris from the stone. Once you've identified the ancestor's stone that you'd like to make a rubbing of, use the brush to lightly clean it off. Once it's tidy, use the masking tape to attach a length of paper over the area you want to rub.

Use the flattest surface of the crayon to cover the most area (which is why a chunk of colored art wax is useful as opposed to a crayon found in your kid's pencil box). Start your rubbing by filling in the outer edges of any carved areas to give yourself a focal point to work toward. Move to the center and begin working outward again toward the edges using light, even strokes without putting too much pressure on the paper or the stone beneath it. If it looks like your rubbing isn't showing up as clearly or well-defined as you'd like, don't fret—you can add more definition later. Just be sure to keep your strokes uniform to avoid any variations in coloring.

As you're making your rubbing, think about the person who is buried there. Offer a prayer of thanks to them, showing your appreciation. It can be complex and deep, or it can be as simple as *Martha Jackson, I celebrate you with this rubbing. Thank you for your contributions to the world and to my life. I welcome you to my home and give you a place of honor on my altar.*

Once you're done, take a moment to step back and look at your rubbing from a distance. If you view it from a few steps away, you'll probably notice some irregularities in the shading or details; this is the time to fix it. When you're satisfied with the end result, carefully remove the tape, and roll up your paper to take home with you—you might even want to bring a cardboard tube to store it in for transport. Be sure to clean up any stray bits of paper or other detritus you've created, and before you leave, present an offering of thanks to the ancestor you're working with. This can be a coin, a drink, flowers, or some other item that is meaningful to you. When you get your rubbing home, frame it and place it on your altar; if it's a large one, hang it on the wall above.

*Note: Some people believe grave rubbings can be destructive to a headstone no matter what precautions are taken. However, because there are also graveyard experts who say that a carefully done rubbing shouldn't do any damage to a headstone in good condition, this is really a matter of personal judgement. If you are concerned about potential damage to a grave, don't do it.

Blend Some Incense for Your Ancestors

There are plenty of types and brands of commercially prepared incense, whether you prefer sticks or cones, just about anywhere. One type of incense that's often overlooked is the loose variety, which is what our people would have used a few hundred—or thousand—years ago, before they could just bop over to the local metaphysical shop on the corner.

The use of incense has been documented in spiritual belief systems all over the world; for ages, people have blended and burned fragrant flowers, plants, and herbs in spiritual settings. Using smoke to send prayers and intentions to the universe is one of the oldest known forms of ceremony. Incense is a powerful way to get your ancestors' attention. The best part is that it's super-easy to make—all you need to get started is a blend of herbs, flowers, resins, wood bark, and berries.

Loose incense is burned either in a fire or on a charcoal disk (you can buy these in packages in any metaphysical shop or even church supply stores). Apply a match to the charcoal —*not* the same charcoal used in a grill—and you'll know it's lit when it begins to spark and glow reddish orange. Once ready, place a pinch of your loose incense on the top of the disk in a fireproof dish.

If you plan to include resins or essential oils in your loose incense, combine them before adding any other materials using a mortar and pestle to mash them until they're nice and gummy. Next add bark or berries, and then dried flowers or herbs or other powdery items last. The following incense recipes are presented in tablespoon measurements, but you can increase it as needed or use a larger measuring unit; just be sure to keep the proportions the same.

Burn these incense blends on your altar during ritual work, or just leave them loose in a bowl to enjoy their fragrances.

Spirit Incense

This incense blend works well for any sort of spirit work. If you're calling upon your ancestors or any other beings for assistance, this combination seems to attract them!

- 1 T dragon's blood resin
- 1 T patchouli oil
- 2 T dried rosemary
- 1 T juniper berries
- 2 T cinnamon
- 1 T ground cloves

Love Blend Incense

Are you doing a working that involves attracting and finding love, strengthening your existing relationships, or celebrating basic family connections? Try burning this love blend on your altar.

- 2 T catnip
- 2 T chamomile blossoms
- 1 T dried rose petals
- 1 T lavender blossoms
- 1 T apple blossoms
- ½ T yarrow

Protection Incense

Sometimes we need protection against outside forces or our own internal nonsense. Use this incense blend when you're asking your ancestors to step in for protective purposes.

- 4 T patchouli
- 3 T lavender
- 1 T mugwort
- 1 T hyssop

Flowers and Plants

Did you know the Victorians had a secret code attached to flowers? Each flower was assigned a meaning, and it was a way to send messages to people—both those you liked and those you didn't. Many of those traditions have held fast, and we still assign meanings to various flowers today. You can add freshly cut flowers to your ancestor altar as a way of sending them a message in the afterlife. Dried flowers are perfectly acceptable too, especially if they came from a funeral wreath or arrangement. Avoid using plastic flowers unless they have a specific meaning to you—the ones that were in your late grandmother's favorite Sunday hat are perfectly acceptable.

Lilies appear at a lot of funerals, partly because they're lovely, but also because they smell amazing. They are symbolic of the innocence of the human soul and tend to evoke feelings of peacefulness. Different strains of lilies have different meanings—a white lily is representative of purity, while a stargazer lily is a show of sympathy.

Roses have a language all their own, typically based on color. In general, roses are associated with love, but red is passionate love while pink is sweeter and more innocent, and yellow is the rose of friendship. A white rose symbolizes new beginnings.

Gardenias are a popular flower in wedding arrangements because they're so fragrant that you can't help but notice them. The gardenia symbolizes happiness and joy, and indicate purity, love, and grace. Interestingly, the gardenia is also associated with clarity and self-reflection; in some magical traditions, they are used for meditative focus to help open the mind to enlightenment.

Flowers aren't the only plants you can use on your altar. Consider some of the herbs you might associate with death and the afterlife. Rosemary is one of the best-known herbs of remembrance; Shakespeare's Ophelia declares it so as she enumerates a list of plants that will ease her emotional anguish. Many cultures also used it for protection from evil spirits. Add a few sprigs of fresh, aromatic rosemary to your altar.

Mugwort is an herb related to divination and dreaming. It's ideal for altar use, especially if you're trying to reach out to your ancestors via meditation; place it under your pillow for lucid dream journeys. You can take sprigs of mugwort and dry them into smudge sticks, and then use it in place of incense for ancestor workings involving guidance and prophecy.

The apple is a symbol of immortality. You can incorporate the dried fruits or the blossoms from a tree into your altar arrangement. Pomegranates can be used in rituals that involve spirit communication, thanks to their prominent role in the story of Demeter and Persephone, in which the seeds are associated with the realm of the underworld. Squashes, pumpkins, and gourds are connected to both protection and psychic awareness.

Rowan branches and berries are used in many parts of the British Isles to keep evil spirits out of the house. If you're doing work with ancestors who might have been questionable or shady, keep some rowan twigs on your altar. The birch is associated with creation and rebirth, particularly after destruction; when a forest burns down, the birch is one of the first trees to come back. Consider writing petitions to your ancestors on birch bark, if they're related to themes of renewal, creativity, and even fertility. The willow, which grows best when there's a lot of rain, is tied to the concepts of healing and growth, and it offers nurturing and protection from danger.

Four

WORKING WITH YOUR BADASS FAMILY

So how do we develop meaningful relationships with our ancestors? Well, obviously we start with the research—that's a big part of it. We learn who they were and how they lived, we study them. It shows them that we're actually investing time and energy in getting to know them. Not only that, we can try to live in a way that shows our reverence and respect for them daily. In doing so, they'll help us out. It's kind of part of the Afterlife Job Description.

One of the best ways to form these relationships with our people is to live in a way that honors them, spiritually. There are a number of ways that you can do this, and all of them will soon become life habits if you practice them regularly.

Live Authentically, With Purpose

For starters, do your best to live as an ethical and loving person. This means, quite simply, make an effort to fulfill your highest potential and find your purpose—whatever it may be—while you're here on earth. Many cultures believe we have a karmic destiny to fulfill, and that we're all just one more link in a cosmic chain. If that is indeed the case, then we honor all of the other links when we make it a priority to do what we need in order to live the most authentic life we can. Your ancestors are your allies—remember their power, and live life to the fullest in their honor. In contrast, when we lose touch with this ancestral power, we can ask our ancestors to help bring about the big changes we need to live our life with purpose.

What do we mean when we talk about authentic living? While it sounds like a totally catchy New Age buzzword, there's actually a sociological concept behind it. Living authentically is a pretty simple idea, and it's focused around the idea that it's perfectly acceptable—and probably far healthier—to live in a way that allows our actions and words to be consistent with our beliefs and values.

Keep in mind that living authentically is a pretty subjective value statement; you're the only one who can decide what's real and authentic for you. But consider this: authentic living is liberating, because once we shed the artifice of worrying about trying to pretend to be something we're not, all that's left is the genuine article. There's a linear progression in finding the true self. Once you've reached that point—or peak, or plateau, depending on your perspective—you've got nothing but authentic living on the road ahead.

How do we get to that state of finding our true selves, when we've spent much of our lives trying to please other people, make everyone happy, fit in, blend, and be part of a society that emphasizes conformity and leaves very little room for individuality? The first step on our journey to authenticity is self-awareness. Define your values and figure out what matters most to you. What are your goals? What things are important, both in your interpersonal relationships and your material life?

Train yourself to be watchful for times when you're *not* being authentic. Did you do or say something that conflicts with your core values? Are you holding others to a standard you don't meet yourself? Pay attention to moments of your own insincerity and try to evaluate what fears might be at their root. Are you worried that someone might dislike or reject you if they see you for your true self?

To develop a mindset of living as your true self, you have to change your way of thinking, not only about yourself, but about the way you interact with others. Let go of patterns, bad habits, and toxic relationships that no longer serve you. Be like Marie Kondo—jettison things that don't bring you joy. If something doesn't make your heart sing, it's time to evaluate whether it's worth keeping. Open your heart and your mind to the idea that you are deserving of love and happiness. You're entitled to receive it, and you're entitled to give it to those who are worthy of you.

Allow your spirit to be free. Do all the things that make you happy, whether it's singing, dancing, or jumping around your living room. Ask strangers if you can pet their dogs. Spend time with people whose company you really enjoy. Make art and music and poetry. If you want to live an empowered life, living an authentic one is the first step, and your ancestors will be proud of you for taking the leap.

Do Good Works

Another thing you can do to honor your family lines is consistently perform positive actions in your ancestors' names. Make donations in their honor (they don't have to be large endowments or actions that create huge financial burdens for you). You could also perform smaller acts that represent who your people were and what they stood for. Two days after my brother-in-law passed away after a lengthy battle with cancer, my teenage son, a regular blood donor at the American Red Cross, contributed a pint of blood in his late uncle's name. I participate in an annual Alzheimer's walk in honor of my maternal grandmother. If you had a family member who did a lot of work with the local food bank, why not organize a drive in her memory? What about the dear aunt who took in all those stray cats? Donate a bag of litter or food to the local feline rescue organization. Here are a few other low-cost charitable actions you can take in honor of your ancestors:

- Handcrafts: Do you knit, crochet, or sew, just like someone in your family did? Assemble blankets, scarves, or hats, and donate them to a homeless shelter or a low-income school in an ancestor's name.

- Donate your time: Most nonprofits are short on volunteers. Contribute your time to an organization that needs your help and represents something that a particular ancestor would have liked to be involved in. Whether you spend a few hours a month shelving books at the library, cleaning cages at the humane society, or scooping food onto trays at a local soup kitchen, do it in a way that honors your people and your guides.

- Raise money for a cause: Donating to your favorite charity organizations can get expensive. Instead, raise funds and awareness on their behalf. Participate in activities like walkathons, charity bike rides, or other community events to collect donations.

- Contribute your skills: What are you good at? Are you a trained grant writer? Do you have mad accounting talent? Can you teach other people how to do something really cool? Offer to help out a local organization by sharing your talents on their behalf. Most nonprofit groups are thrilled when someone shows up and says, *I'm a professional Whatever, and I'd love to help you out by Whatevering for your organization.*

There is a definite spiritual benefit of performing acts of generosity. By giving to help others' well-being, we increase our own well-being. If you think of it in the context of the adages *you get back what you give* or *like attracts like,* you can see how generosity is weirdly paradoxical, something that is true in nearly every spiritual path.

In the Christian religion, charity and good works are part of the trajectory to grace. Islam has a practice known as *sadaqah,* the act of giving charity or alms to another without any expectation of return other than to please Allah. The concept of *tzedekah* in Judaism includes not only morally upright behavior but also the call to give generously; material support for those who might need it isn't just a suggestion or guideline, it's a requirement. The Hindu and Buddhist *dāna* is not just the act of giving itself; it's also the desire to give from the heart without any demands for repayment from the recipient.

Traditional and indigenous practices of many cultures often place special emphasis on the benefits of sharing blessings and abundance. In other words, if your people have been benevolent to you, pay it forward to others. While we could argue that acts of charity make us feel good about ourselves, and are therefore self-serving, the fact remains that there are scientific studies which show that generosity is also good for us physically; it can lower blood pressure and reduce levels of stress.

Listen to Your Heart

Stay open to communication from your kinfolk—sometimes it's direct, and other times it's non-verbal. While ritual itself often brings about contact, it can also happen spontaneously in dreams, through symbols, or via other messages. When we're willing to hear what our ancestors are saying, it makes their work easier, and we get to enjoy the relationship we develop with them. In chapter 5, you'll learn how to do rituals that will help you talk to your people so you'll know how to speak with them, but here are a few key things to keep in mind:

- Follow the same etiquette you might use if you're speaking to a living person—take the time to introduce yourself. *Hi, I'm Samantha, daughter of James and Jasmine, and I'm really happy to meet you.*

- Remember that just as you speak casually to one group of people in your life, you might speak more thoughtfully and formally to another. Think about how your ancestors may like you to speak with them—should you say *I call upon my people, known and unknown, going back through generations?* Or, realistically, would they prefer *Hey guys, it's me. Need some help, y'all!* as your introduction?

- Sometimes, we don't know what to say at all, but we still need to speak. In those cases, it's perfectly fine to just start talking. *Grandma, I know you'd love this joke I heard,* or *Aunt Margaret, you are not going to believe what Ethel Sanderson told me about Cousin Alex the other day!* Have conversations, either aloud or in your head. Talk to them in a way that shows you're ready to develop a relationship.

In addition to speaking to your people, you have to teach yourself to listen to them in return. So, how do you do that? First of all, you'll probably question your sanity and start wondering if you're really getting these messages, but just hear me out. After all, we've all been to the movies—we know people think you're nuts if you start whispering, *I hear dead people.* But hearing your ancestors is primarily intuitive. Much of their communication with you will be nonverbal, in that there won't be an audible conversation…but you'll still *hear* them.

Make sure you're working with evolved and benevolent ancestors and not manipulative entities. Ask your ancestral guides to give you feedback on other beings you might be working with to make sure you can trust them and that they have your best interests at heart.

How do you know that you're working with a real ancestor spirit and not just some random being—or worse yet, your own fanciful imagination? Well, the more you speak to your ancestors, the more you'll notice patterns. Some will speak formally, others more casually. You have to trust your instinct, and it's just as important to use some basic critical thinking skills as you're getting to know them.

When I first began doing ancestor work, I discovered that my people were the ones who would pop in and tell me things that I *needed* to hear but didn't necessarily *want* to hear. Here's an example. Let's say you're doing some work in which you call upon a long-dead ancestor and you're trying to develop a relationship with them…and they ask you to prepare their favorite food and place it on their altar. Unfortunately, their favorite food is something you don't know how to cook and don't want to learn how to prepare, for whatever reason. My paternal ancestors are Scottish, so there's a lot of potential there for someone to demand I fix a plate of haggis.

Now, I've never made haggis. I don't want to make haggis. I'm repulsed by the very *idea* of haggis, a sheep's stomach stuffed with oats and a bunch of other things that were eaten in Scotland a few centuries back. I'm pretty sure it would smell terrible if I made one, and I don't want my house to carry the aroma of haggis. But if I was calling on one of my MacFarlane or McFadyen or Kerr or MacKie ancestors and they demanded haggis, I'd learn how to make it, and I'd put it on my altar for them.

Are your people asking for things you don't even like? That's a good sign it's not your imagination. Because if I got a request for a batch of my amazing homemade peanut butter chocolate chip cookies (pretty much a twentieth century treat), I would know it probably wasn't my kinfolk calling but my own desire for some butt-kicking chocolate chip cookies.

You may encounter your ancestors via dream visitation; even skeptics sometimes get visits in their dreams—especially once you've set up an ancestor altar and begun researching your people and learning their stories. Sure, your grandmother's been dead since 1973, but that doesn't mean she can't pop in and check on you. Don't be shocked if she—and other kinfolk—start appearing to you while you sleep. They might speak to you in your dreams, or they may simply watch over you. The key is that if they *do* seem to have something to say, pay attention. You may find it helpful to keep a notepad by your bed so that when you wake up, you can jot things down—even if it's just *Uncle Herb says to get my act together*—before you forget. Record now, interpret later.

If you feel as though you truly met and spoke with your kinfolk in a dream, you probably did. Meeting ancestors in this way can often help with healing generational trauma; if pain runs in the family, you have the power to make it run out. Offer to work with any ancestors for healing purposes if they seem to be in distress. Offer to help with reparations for those who seem as though they need to atone for the misdeeds perpetuated during their lifetimes.

You might also find that as you're holding photos of your people or heirlooms or other items, you hear a voice that's not really a voice or words that aren't really being spoken … and yet are real. One moment you're dusting off a photo of Great Aunt Agnes, and the next moment, there's a soft voice murmuring *Thank you* that's as clear as day, even though no one else in the room has heard it. Don't dismiss these as your own imagination. Instead, acknowledge them and let them know you've listened to what was said.

Finally, don't discount the value of symbols, signs, and omens. Did you suddenly get a whiff of tobacco smoke out of the blue as you sat down for breakfast? Maybe it's that one ancestor who always smoked a pipe in the mornings as he read his paper. Perhaps you keep seeing the number seventeen wherever you go … could it be a sign from your great-great-uncle the riverboat gambler, who claimed seventeen was his lucky number?

Calling Your Ancestors as Badass Spirit Guides

If you've tried talking to your ancestors, set up the altar, done the research, and are *still* having trouble connecting to them, don't worry. It doesn't always happen overnight. One thing you can do is specifically invite them in to be your guides. In this sense, they are guides—ancestral spirits who are there to *guide,* not offer protection from your crappy neighbor, help you win the lottery, or mess around with healing your various medical issues. Often, asking for a guide is a good way to get started with ancestor work, because it's sort of a low-pressure way for you to get to know each other. So how do you find your ancestral spirit guides? A lot of times, it's just a matter of opening up to them—remember, most people in the Western world grow up thinking this sort of thing is nonsense, so you have to train yourself to suspend the disbelief you've been conditioned to.

Start by welcoming your natural intuitive gifts. Everyone has them to some degree, but some of us are more aware than others. Have you ever heard that soft little whisper in your head that tells you it's time to do something, even though it makes no real sense to you? Take the north freeway to work instead of the southern one, make a big change in your life even though it's scary, or just sit back and pay attention to the things people *don't* say to you...all of these are things that your intuition may be telling you, and so often, we just dismiss it with *I must be crazy for thinking this*. It's possible that this intuitive voice is actually the presence of a spirit guide, and it could well be an ancestor popping in. Learn to evaluate your intuitive ideas and see if they work out for you. If they do, it may well be an ancestral guide talking to you.

Some people find ancestral guides using meditation. While there are a number of guided meditations you can do to meet your guides available commercially, you can also connect with them by meditating on your own. As you begin, clear your mind of anything that's not related to meeting your guides; you may want to light some incense or play some soft, non-intrusive music in the background.

For many people, this meditation takes the form of a long, solitary journey. Visualize yourself walking in a remote place, far from the crowds and technology and your job and your cell phone. Maybe you're on a path wending through a forest, or on a trail traversing a craggy mountainside, or surrounded by tall grasses out in the steppes of eastern Russia. As you wander along the trail, allow yourself to look around, and you'll often meet someone along the way—and this person could be your ancestral guide. Often, guides appear as representative archetypes—that means they can be someone who symbolizes other things. If your guide looks like Eleanor Roosevelt, that doesn't necessarily mean Eleanor herself *is* your ancestral guide, but she may represent a person who wants to share certain things with you—honesty, leadership, discipline, and so on.

Much like meditation, a lucid dream journey is a way you can meet your guide or guides through the work of your subconscious. However, unlike in meditation, you're actually asleep during a lucid dream journey. Lucid dreaming is dreaming with a purpose, so as you tuck in for the night, start thinking about what you want to dream about—in this case, focus on meeting an ancestral guide. Allow this to be the last—and only—thing you think about as you fall asleep. Lucid dreaming can be a challenge if you've never done it before, but once you get the hang of it, you'll be able to pre-plan your dream journey, and what you might be doing on your adventures. Because most of us forget our dreams shortly after waking, it's important to write down any messages you get during a lucid dream journey as soon as you're coherent enough to pick up a pen. Include information about anyone you happen to meet; go back later and evaluate your notes for meanings, symbols, and patterns.

Speaking of symbols and patterns, we often look for these things when they aren't there ... and then fail to recognize it when they're right in front of our faces. Some guides might decide to make themselves known to you—especially if they've got some important tea to spill—with a series of signs and symbols. These symbols can be very basic—perhaps you keep seeing owls, and you've never noticed them before, but you just found out that your 4th great-grandmother raised barn owls in her spare time. Signs and symbols can also be more complex and detailed, which will require a bit of self-analysis in addition to figuring out how those patterns connect to ancestors—including those who are yet undiscovered.

Many people believe that if you want real answers from your guides, you have to actually ask them something—and you may have to present the question more than once. Don't just assume your people are going to spoon-feed you with information because you want them to. Ask a question—or for a solution—then watch for signs or omens that provide an answer.

Finally, consider doing a bit of psychic divination. Most people want to discover their ancestral guides on their own—it's a pretty personal thing—so if you're skilled at divination, you can try your favorite methods yourself to see if you can contact a guide or guides. However, if none of the above methods have really proved effective despite your best efforts, you can ask a friend with psychic skills to do a bit of divination on your behalf. A talented psychic— and this doesn't have to be a professional psychic, it can be anyone whose intuitive gifts you trust—can see if you've got guides around you and often can help you identify them.

Remember, not all of your guides are going to appear at once, and you may find them showing up in turns. Once you discover your ancestral guides, they may not all be available to you all the time —after all, they're busy, just like you are. Sometimes they wait to appear until they're needed— after all, the purpose of a guide is to guide you. If you're doing okay without them for a while, they might be off helping others who need it more than you do. Keep in mind that you may not be their only descendant who needs a hand.

What Can Your People Do for You?

Your ancestors are there to offer help. They can show up with nuggets of wisdom garnered throughout the centuries, transcending generations, and give insight when you need it—but again, you sometimes have to request it.

Ask for guidance from your ancestors. Trust me, they've seen it all, and they've probably got plenty of ideas about what you've done and what comes next. If you're stuck, invite them to come in and help you problem-solve. I have a couple of very specific ancestors that I've discovered are really good at critical thinking. They help me look at a problem objectively, break it down into all of its individual components, and then guide me to evaluate my different choices and all of the possible outcomes of each decision. It's a bit like having a team with a flow chart pointing out *If this, then that* for me, but it works incredibly well, and they've never steered me wrong.

Thank your ancestors for good things that have happened. Remember, in a lot of cultures it's believed that if you've been the beneficiary of good fortune, it's because your ancestral guides are watching out for you. Remember when you were a child, and you wrote thank you notes to people who gave you gifts? Write a thank you letter to those ancestors, either collectively or individually. It could be complex and detailed, or as short and simple as:

> Dear Aunt Martha,
>   Thank you for giving me the wisdom and strength
> to make the right choices.
>   I appreciate all you have done for me.

After you've written a letter to your people, bury it near a place of family significance or burn it in a small bowl or cauldron on your altar.

Ask your badass ancestors for protection. They have a vested interest in keeping an eye on you that extends to other living members of your family. When you call upon them and invite them into your home, it becomes their home as well, and they're far more likely to keep a watchful eye upon it.

It's perfectly okay to ask your ancestors for financial assistance. How you do this will vary, but there are traditions all around the world in which ancestors are petitioned to grant material blessings upon their living descendants. In China, there's a custom called spirit money. Practitioners write their ancestor's name on joss paper or extra bills, and then burn it at the altar to send them money in the afterlife. In return, money comes back to the living in abundance.

No matter how you choose to work with your blood kinfolk, above all, honor them. Celebrate them. Take the time to show them that they matter, even in death, to those who still live. Again, the *how* of ancestor work will depend on your belief system. If you're Catholic, you may use rosary prayers, or if you were raised Baptist you may have devotionals more in line with your beliefs and practices. How often you tend your ancestor altar will vary as well. It's up to you to decide the proper form the veneration of your ancestors takes—just make sure that it fits with who they are and what they expect from you.

For most who begin spiritual ancestor work, the establishing of a ritualized format becomes a long-term habit. What I typically do before I start with any other ancestor work—is light my candles and then offer an opening prayer. I use the same one almost every time; it's a short part of a longer Gaelic prayer that the old ones in the Scottish Highlands are said to use before they do the rest of their spiritual work. It gets me in the right frame of mind to do whatever else it is I have to focus on with my ancestral guides.

An suil an Athar a chruthaich mi,
An suil an Mhithar a chruthaich mi,
An suil an Spioraid a chruthaich mi.
In the eye of the Father who created me,
In the eye of the Mother who created me,
In the eye of the Spirit who created me.

Your opening prayer—in whatever form it may take—can be followed by an invitation welcoming your ancestors into your home. Address them by name and ask them to commune with you, be cared for by you, and to share their gifts of wisdom, protection, and guidance to you, your home, and your living family members. When you've finished whatever work you need to do, thank your ancestors for stopping by—and remember, even if you didn't get the answers you had hoped for, you likely got the answers you needed to hear.

Stepping Outside the Gender Norms

For those of us living in the 21st century, there's far more open discussion about gender, sexuality, and binaries than there was for our ancestors, even those who lived just a generation or two ago. We're talking about privilege, about heteronormative cultural mores, in today's world, and we're doing it in a way that the generations before us probably wouldn't have understood. However, that doesn't mean that all of those people from centuries gone by were constrained by the boundaries of their assigned gender roles.

If you're someone who's something other than a cisgender heterosexual person, you may find it comforting to know that transitioning into the spirit realm can sometimes be helpful for ancestors who were unable to embrace their true gender identity in life.

Even if you *are* a cisgender heterosexual person, you'll probably encounter long-dead kinfolk who identify with any number of spots along the LGBTQ spectrum. You may discover that navigating their queer or nonbinary or trans or whatever identity got a whole lot more manageable for them once they were no longer constrained by the social norms of their time and place in life.

Consider for a moment that it's a fairly recent idea that our gender isn't based on body parts at all, and that the parts and plumbing we're born with don't have to be predictors of our personal life or our professional path. We've figured out that it's unhealthy to force people to conform to traditional gender stereotypes if our authentic selves need and want to travel along another path. Whether you're a woman who exists in a professional space that's traditionally masculine, a man who has hobbies considered traditionally feminine, someone who was assigned female at birth but lives as male (or vice versa) or a person who identifies with both genders or none at all, there's room at the table for you in many facets of modern society.

Not so for our ancestors. For much of the human timeline, certain roles based upon assigned gender were the standard expectation. Women were conditioned to grow up and marry, have children, and raise them, all while following proper decorum and behaving in ways that were seen as *feminine*. For men, the path consisted of traditionally *masculine* roles—working, supporting a family, being the breadwinner. Women were taught to be passive and obedient and pretty, while men were raised to take up whatever space they're in, be dominant, and strong.

But imagine for a minute what it might have been like for an ancestor in the past—maybe not that distant, either—who wanted to break those boundaries, for women who were loud and boisterous and confident and took up space ... who might be considered *mannish?* What about a man who would rather paint or dance than go hunting for sport, who could be called a *fop* or a *dandy?* What about that ancestor a few centuries or even a few decades ago who had to hide who they were because they were born in the wrong body or because their queerness—that today we'd encourage them to embrace—was a criminal offense punishable by hanging?

Trust me, some of your people are existing in the afterlife on the wide-ranging branches of the nonconformity tree, and it's incredibly important that you acknowledge and respect that. No matter how you identify yourself on the gender spectrum, your ancestors were who they were—and there will be more than a few who are going to let you know about it, once you start working with them. They may pop in and say *Oh, by the way, I'm claiming my spot as part of the queer community.* If you get a hint that the great-something grandmother who had two husbands and nine children actually preferred the company of women, let her run with it and honor that part of her that was likely kept hidden throughout her lifetime.

If you yourself are gender-nonconforming, then working with these ancestors can be healing and beneficial for both you *and* them—because they may want a chance to finally live authentically, in a way that they couldn't in their own time and place; they may wish to do so by celebrating through you and your experiences. However, it's also crucial to *listen* to what your ancestors are telling you—they may prefer to keep their gender identity private, thanks to their own history, as well as the social and cultural norms of the time and place in which they lived. It's not up to us to force anyone out of the closet, living or dead, if they indicate their stories are not ours to share.

Working with Historical Figures

At some point during your genealogical excursions, there's a good chance you're going to run into someone famous—or infamous, depending on your people's propensity for bad behavior. In a way, this can be a super-lucky find, because if they're famous, you'll be able to find a ton of research on them that's already been done. The downside, however, is that you'll be able to find a ton of research that's already been done—in other words, you're going to be reading about their pitfalls and bad habits right along with their good ones. Take this with a grain of salt—just like living people, dead ones were human too. They made mistakes, got sloppy and careless, and sometimes lived in a way that was less than honorable. It's who we are, as a species.

If you've managed to trace your family tree back to any of England's aristocracy, it can make for some pretty interesting dinner table conversation, but remember that most people of European descent who are alive today are genetically tied to the kings of England, simply because genetics are a numbers game. In 2013, a pair of geneticists, Peter Ralph and Graham Coop, did a study showing that anyone who was alive and left descendants in the ninth century is the ancestor of everyone living in Europe now. Take Charlemagne, the Carolingian King of the Franks and Holy Roman Emperor, for instance. He's my 35th great-grandfather... but he was also the father of at least twenty children, and the great ancestor of around *a trillion people* over the twelve centuries since his death. That's a lot of descendants, and we're all genetically connected, which means if one of us is special because we're related to someone famous, then we're *all* special. If we're *all* special... well, you get the idea.

I've got other famous people in my tree—again, mostly thanks to the European royalty connection—and they're not all in a direct line. I've got William the Conqueror and his great-something grandfather as well as Rollo the Viking, who laid siege to Paris. King Edward Longshanks and the kings of Scotland are in my direct lines, and a couple of America's founding fathers and Abraham Lincoln are tied into my family through a complex web of cousins, marriages, and cousin marriages. I've quite possibly got one of the scandalous Chicago Black Sox of 1919, although that one still isn't confirmed. I have saints and popes thrown in there for good measure—the great irony is that I've never been Christian, or anything even remotely close to it, but I still work with these people on occasion.

The point is that I treat them like any other ancestor I would work with or call upon. No one gets a pass just because they're a historically well-known figure. While it's easy to get excited about famous ancestors and see them through rose-colored glasses, hold them to the same standards you would hold the pioneers, the farmers, the blacksmiths, the scullery maids, the paupers, and everyone else who didn't get a special on the History Channel.

When You Just Can't Even

You may find yourself not wishing to work with blood family members, ever, for any reason. There are any number of possibilities—perhaps you've got Problem Ancestors or people who have perpetuated cycles of abuse, bigotry, and violence. Whatever your rationale behind it, that's completely your decision—don't ever let anyone tell you that you absolutely *must* do ancestor work or you're obviously not a True Pagan.

In addition to giving you life—admittedly, a bit of a problematic and heteronormative concept—your ancestors may have given you a legacy of terror and pain. Perhaps you grew up in a family where violence was the norm rather than the exception. Maybe your people were cold and distant, and emotions were something that only the weak showed. Did you grow up in a family group whose religious principles made it nearly impossible for you to feel loved and accepted? In cases where blood family is a problem for you, consider working with archetypes instead, covered in chapter 8.

Five

RITUALS AND MEDITATIONS FOR YOUR KIN

You've researched and learned, figured out who your people are, and you've even given them their own space with an altar. Great job!

But now what?

Now it's time to really start working with them. There are endless numbers of ways you can do this, but we're going to dive right in with meditations, rituals, craft projects, and even meal ideas to celebrate your family's heritage in a way that does your ancestors honor. With any of the prayers, petitions, or rituals included here, they're written with the generic and group-encompassing term *ancestors*, but you can modify them if you want to address a specific person in your badass kin collection. Feel free to call upon individuals rather than the collective whole if it's more appropriate for your intent and purpose.

Badass Ancestor Protection Ritual

This is a simple protection ritual which invites your ancestors to be your badass security detail for you, your family, and your home. Although they'll feel a bit protective of you anyway, simply by virtue of your working with them at your altar space, you can directly ask them to step in as metaphysical guardians when you need them. This ritual is a bit martial in nature, so if you feel like you need something a little more gentle and polite—maybe your ancestors are more dignified than mine—feel free to adapt it as needed.

To call upon your ancestors to protect your home, and all that dwell inside it, do this ritual outside your house. You'll need four iron railroad spikes, one for each corner of the yard, and a beverage to use as an offering. Start at the edge of the property nearest your front door and begin moving clockwise around your home along the perimeter. If you live in an apartment or dormitory, or you think your neighbors will be weirded out, you can always do this inside as needed, but you won't be able to pound the spikes into the floor; instead, use small iron nails and leave them in the corners of your home. As you walk the edge of your yard, ask your ancestors to watch over the place:

> *Hail, my kinfolk! Hail, my clan!*
> *Hail, those who came before me!*
> *Protect my home, protect my people, protect my property!*
> *Ancestors, this is your home as well—*
> *guard over me and all those I love!*

As you reach each corner of the yard, pound one of the railroad spikes into the soil. Iron is associated with protection in many cultures, and this will help create a metaphysical boundary against troublemakers who might want to cause you harm. When you pound each spike in, remind your ancestors that you belong to them.

> *Hail, my ancestors, guardians of this home!*
> *Let none enter that would do me harm,*
> *And may this home and family fall under your protection!*

Pour the beverage over the soil where you've pounded the spike, as an offering, and say, *Ancestors, I give you this drink of coffee/ whisky/wine to show my gratitude for your watchful eyes. I thank you.*

Move to each corner of the yard, repeating the process: pour out a bit of the beverage for your ancestors as you pound the spikes into the ground. When you return to your starting point, offer a final thanks:

> *Hail, my kinfolk! Hail, my clan!*
> *Hail, those who came before me!*
> *This home and family are under your protection,*
> *Hail, my kinfolk! Hail, my clan!*
> *Hail, those who came before me!*
> *I thank you for standing guard.*

Take a small scoop of soil from your front yard, place it in a jar with a lid, and keep it on your ancestor altar to help strengthen your property's connection to your kin.

Meditation to Call upon Unknown Kinfolk

If you're trying to connect with ancestors whose names you don't know, don't sweat it. There's no reason you can't reach out to them. Look at it this way. If there was someone you saw regularly, at school or work or in your community, and you wanted to get to know them, the best way to find out who they are is to just talk to them. This simple meditation can be used to call unknown ancestors into your life.

Begin by lighting your favorite incense and place a series of three plain white candles on your altar. If you normally cast a circle or cleanse your space before meditating, this is the time to do it. Sit comfortably in front of your altar. Close your eyes and clear your mind. Eliminate everything mundane from your thoughts—stop worrying about the dog's upcoming visit to the vet, or whether you took enough chicken out of the freezer for tomorrow's dinner. Focus only on your inner light. Imagine a soft glow, forming at your heart, and slowly pulsing, beating with the love of a hundred generations. Imagine that light spreading outward, gradually enveloping your entire body, from your head to your toes, beginning at the crown chakra and shimmering all the way down to your feet.

Imagine this light as a cloak that your ancestors have wrapped you in, sending you their love and power across the centuries. When you're ready to begin, light the first white candle. Focus on the flame, and say, *Hail my people, those unknown, those still nameless, those yet undiscovered. I call to you, inviting you to this sacred space. Reveal to me who you are, in names and actions and words.*

Listen carefully as you call them in. Ask for their names—do certain ones come to mind, perhaps Nathaniel or Keziah or Abigail? Can you see their images, maybe an elderly woman in a turban, a man in a soldier's outfit, or a child standing beside a mountain hut?

Light the second candle. Call out, *Hail my people, those unknown, those still nameless, those yet undiscovered. I call to you, inviting you to this sacred space. Show me the strength you bring to my bloodline.*

Now that you've called your unknown people in, it's time to see what they've done. Let your mind wander as you associate those names and images with actions and challenges. Can you see someone who is standing up for themselves, or living authentically and bravely? Is there someone that you feel has managed to overcome adversity and oppression? Allow your ancestor guides to lead you down whatever trail they want to take you; they are sharing their story with you.

Finally, light the third candle. Say, *Hail my people, those unknown, those still nameless, those yet undiscovered. I call to you, inviting you to this sacred space. Share with me your wisdom and knowledge.*

Your guides have revealed to you who they are and what they did, and now it's time to invite them to show you what they knew. Ask them to contribute to the collective knowledge of the family, sharing insight and wisdom and lessons learned. When they have finished speaking to you, bid them farewell, and thank them for their time.

Simple Gratitude Prayer for the Ancestors

Want to just take a moment to thank your people for the blessings and gifts they've bestowed upon you? This simple gratitude prayer can be offered at your altar. Begin by making an offering of clean, fresh water, wine, or whatever beverage your kinfolk seem to prefer. As you place your offering upon the altar, close your eyes, and imagine all of your ancestors surrounding you, watching you with pride, and sharing their strength and wisdom with you. Light a candle for each ancestor or specific family line you wish to thank. Say,

I am wrapped in the knowledge you give me
Empowered by the strength you give me
Surrounded by the love you give me
Blessed by all you give me
My gratitude is beyond measure
Greater than seven waves
Taller than seven mountains
Brighter than seven stars
I owe you a debt of family honor
For all the years past

And all the years present
And all the years future
I will pay this forward
For the generations to come
For the legacy of kin
For our family's heritage
And I give you thanks

Ancestor Money Paper Ritual

Okay, so you feel a little weird asking your ancestors for money. Lots of us do—it's always awkward when you have to go to your parents or cousins for some extra cash to tide you over. But you shouldn't feel bad about asking your ancestors for financial aid, because they want you to be successful. Your good fortune reflects well on the whole family, even those members who have been dead for a while.

This type of ritual is found in magical traditions all over the world, under a number of different names. Some call it simply ancestor money, others spirit money or ghost money. No matter what you call it, it's a great way to honor your people and encourage them to send financial blessings back to the realm of the living.

For this ritual, you'll need to figure out which ancestor—or ancestors—you'd like to call upon. Ideally, you'd select someone who might be associated with material blessings. Did you have a rich uncle who died before you were born? Have you traced your genealogy back to a king or wealthy countess in England? Was there a great-grandparent who loved to visit the horse races and always seemed to have extra change in his pockets?

Select the person or people you want to work with and write their name on a paper bill. While you don't want to go broke doing this ritual—after all, you want money coming *to* you, not going *from* you—it's best to use the largest denomination you can afford to spare. If it's a ten or twenty, great. If all you can afford is a single dollar, that's okay too—your ancestors know. In some magical traditions, there is a specific type of paper that's used for this; in Chinese spirituality, names are written on joss paper. If you can find paper money from the time or place that your ancestors lived, that's even better, although it may be worth far more than the face value amount.

As you write the person's name, say, *This is for Lady Mary Howland, my 17th great aunt, that she may have bounty and plenty in the afterlife.* If you'd rather not work with a specific individual, write your collective ancestry—*all of my ancestors*—on the bill, saying, *This is for my ancestors, known and unknown, that they might have bounty and plenty in the afterlife.*

You'll need a small cast iron cauldron or other fire-safe dish for the next part. Light a corner of the paper and burn the money in the cauldron. As it burns, imagine you are opening a door to find your ancestors behind it. Visualize them receiving the money from your hands. Picture them acknowledge your offering—they may be smiling, nodding, or beaming with pride at your efforts. Once the bill has completely burned away, thank your ancestors and close the door. What goes around will soon come around, and money will come your way.

Bountiful Blessings Ritual

Maybe burning a bit of spirit money isn't quite specific enough for you. Perhaps you want to bring abundance your way for a specific purpose. Maybe you want to bring in enough money to pay off your student loans, or to buy a house. Perhaps you've always wanted to own your own business but can't quite get enough capital together. Maybe you just want to get to a point of being debt-free so you can start saving for the future. All of these are perfectly valid reasons for your ancestors to step in—after all, when you achieve your goals and dreams, it reflects well upon the family as a whole.

For this ritual, you're going to get really specific because you're going to write a petition to your ancestors. Essentially, you're going to tell them what you need and why you need it, and then you're going to wrap up with why they should help you get it. Ideally, it's a good idea to do this ritual during the waxing moon phase—the period before the full moon—because that's the time associated with abundance and drawing things towards you.

Although you don't have to do this on paper money as with the previous working, you should make this special—remember how your ancestor altar should look nice because you're inviting your people in as guests? The same is true for your petition: don't write your message on a dirty, crumpled up cocktail napkin you found when cleaning out your car. Take some time with this one. When you were a kid in school, you probably got graded on your penmanship. Do your best work for your ancestors. If you have a specific bill you want to pay off, write your petition on a copy of an invoice or something that represents the thing you need money for—a photo of the house you want to buy, or a copy of the business plan you've drawn up.

Here are some ways a petition can be written:

- I need $15,432 to pay off my student loans, and once they're paid off, I'll use my degree to do something that helps people.

- I need $1,800 to put a down payment on a rental space so I can open the spiritual shop I've always dreamed of, and when I do, I will keep a community altar in place so that others can benefit.

- I need $4,000 so I can travel to Kenya to visit the village my people came from, and when I am there, I will make an offering in your honor.

Once you've written your petition, place it on your ancestor altar. Show it to your ancestors, read it aloud to them. Let them know how important it is to you, and offer an invocation:

I call forth my ancestors, kith and kin, and my spirit is open to receive the bounty you might bestow upon me. My heart is open to share the gifts you might send my way. I ask not from greed but from need, and will use this money to fulfill my greater purpose. I will give back what I can by paying it forward, and keeping myself grounded and whole. I will honor all of you by living in a way that celebrates our family and will make you proud of me. I will honor all of you by living authentically and doing the work you ask of me in return. I will honor all of you as you honor me, and will celebrate your bountiful blessings with gratitude.

Leave your petition on your altar for a full moon cycle and keep an eye out for potential financial changes. When you start seeing income trickle in, be sure to go back to your altar and thank your ancestors for what they've sent your way.

Ancestor Labyrinth Meditation

One of the best-known symbols of balance is the labyrinth. Unlike a maze, which leads us in twists and turns, to dead ends and false stops, a labyrinth is designed to have a beginning, a center, and an end, much like life itself. The labyrinth often becomes a magical geometric shape that lies somewhere between the mundane and the sacred. In some magical and Pagan belief systems, the labyrinth represents the return of the Goddess from the cold darkness of winter to the fertile season of spring. The labyrinth is also a highly useful meditative tool, and when you invite your ancestors in to join you there, it can be extremely powerful.

Labyrinths and images of them have been found at sites dating back thousands of years; at some point, it's very likely your kinfolk walked through one. The most typical style is the seven-circuit Cretan labyrinth, named for the legendary labyrinth of King Minos at Crete. In 2005, a pair of Cretan labyrinth carvings were found etched in cliff faces near Tintagel, Cornwall, England. Their origins have not yet been determined, although they may have been carved any time between the Bronze Age and the nineteenth century.

During the period of the Crusades, families often built a labyrinth as a way to represent the pilgrimage to the Holy Land, and the Chartres design—a fourfold design with eleven circuits—saw a rise in popularity as a status symbol for the well-off. Churches often incorporated the unicursal patterns into floors in their chapels as an earthly representation of worshippers' paths to heaven. This pattern could be walked or crawled, traveled quickly or slowly, and allowed those who were penitent to walk the fine line between the misery of their earthly lives and the joys they believed awaited them in holy salvation.

Later, labyrinths took on a less spiritual and far more playful meaning—wealthy landowners were known to commission labyrinth gardens with high hedges as a place for romantic assignations. Simple unicursal labyrinths were replaced by complex mazes, which forced travelers to make choices and decisions, occasionally pushing them into dead ends from which they were forced to turn back. A labyrinth's purpose is not to misdirect us or cause us to get lost (which a maze is designed to do) but instead the opposite—to help us find our way. Though we may feel a bit confused because of the turns and winding circuits in a labyrinth—almost as though we are walking between the worlds—we're always on the path to the center. Once we reach it, we're always headed towards the exit, and the end of our journey will end with a feeling of harmony and balance.

Labyrinths may be found all over the world. If you have an opportunity to walk one, you can use this simple technique as a problem-solving meditation. If you don't have an actual labyrinth to walk, that's okay—draw or print out an image of one and trace it with your finger while visualizing yourself taking steps through the spirals.

As you enter the labyrinth, walk slowly and evenly. Call your ancestors to you—out loud, or if other people are around, silently. You can enumerate your ancestors individually or invoke them with a simple chant, like *Blood of my blood, bone of my bone, I call my kin to me, heart and home.*

Imagine them walking beside you, generation after generation, as you make your way along the twisting and winding path to the middle of the labyrinth. As you approach the center, visualize whatever dilemma it is you'd like to resolve, and think about how it has been affecting you. Is it a problem of your own making? Are your issues the results of other people's actions, or circumstances beyond your control? How does it make you feel? How has it impacted not only your life, but the lives of those you love and interact with on a daily basis? Explain your quandary to your ancestors as you slowly walk. Have a conversation with them just as you would with living relatives you were asking for advice and guidance.

When you reach the center, it's time to focus on solutions. As you stand in the center of the labyrinth, open yourself up to possible ways of solving your problem, and ask your ancestors what they would do. The center is a location of true balance, a space between the worlds—neither the path of entrance nor the way to the exit—and this, for many people, is a perfect place to find resolution. Figure out what steps would have to be taken to enact a solution to the problem. Will it be a multi-pronged approach, involving other people? Is it a simple quick fix that you never would have thought of on your own?

Finally, as you work your way slowly out of the labyrinth, back to the beginning, think about how things will change for you once you get your solutions in place. What guidance do your ancestors have for you? Can they help you make sure you don't end up repeating old and unhealthy habits? Consider how your life will be different when your problem has been solved.

Ritual to Appreciate Your People

This ritual is one that serves as a great way to just show your gratitude for your ancestors. Start by tidying up your ancestor altar—you should always keep it clean, but this is a good opportunity to freshen it up a little. Replace or clean the altar cloth, dust all the nooks and crannies and picture frames. Change out the water or other beverage you have as an offering. Add newly cut flowers or other organic items that you might have sitting around your altar. Add a large candle at the center of the altar for this ritual. You'll also want seven smaller candles, ideally white; tealights or plain votives are perfect for this.

Begin by taking a moment to think about all the things you have to be thankful for. What aspects of your ancestors have you benefited from? Perhaps you've been gifted with a family knack for being skilled at crafts, or you're genetically predisposed to being long-lived and healthy. Maybe you inherited a love of science or math from someone in your family, or you're actively working to expand your late grandfather's stamp collection as a labor of love. Did someone amass a fortune that has allowed you to live comfortably? These are just a few things to consider—ask yourself what gifts your ancestors have bestowed upon you over the course of your lifetime.

Light the larger candle and focus on the flame. As you do, call out to the ancestors you wish to thank, and tell them *why* you appreciate them. *Tonight, I celebrate you and honor you, my kin and blood. I honor great-grandmother Lorena, who lived in a dirt-floor cabin and taught me to make the best biscuits I've ever had. I honor Cousin Marcus, the first in my family to go to college, who inspired my love of history. I honor my tenth great-grandfather, Nathaniel, who started a printing press and spoke out against tyranny and unjust rulers.*

Make an offering to show your appreciation. It should be something you've made yourself or that has great sentimental value. As you present it, tell your ancestors how much their legacy means to you. *I give you this gift of homemade bread, kneaded by my own hands, so that you may never hunger in the afterlife, and I thank you for the gifts you have given me.* Or, *I present you with this shawl I knit myself, calling upon you for guidance with my needles, and I am grateful for the skills I have inherited from you.*

As you reflect upon your people, allow yourself to open up with gratitude. Send those feelings of thankfulness out into the universe, across the many generations going back in your family tree, sharing it with your people. Begin lighting the seven smaller candles. As you light each of them, say,

> *One candle to thank my grandmothers.*
> *A second candle to thank my grandfathers.*
> *Three candles to thank my aunts.*
> *Four candles to thank my uncles.*
> *A fifth candle to thank my cousins.*
> *This sixth candle to thank all of my ancestors,*
> *and the seventh to let you know someday I will join you*
> *and I will take my place beside you,*
> *and I will thank you for the honor.*

Continue sending out your gratitude to your ancestors and allow the candles to burn out on their own. Leave your offering in place for twenty-four hours before moving it or disposing of it.

Ancestor Healing Ritual

This is a short ritual you can do to ask your ancestors to step in and aid with healing and wellness. After all, if you're healthy and whole, physically and emotionally and mentally, you're far better able to do credit to your family line—again, your ancestors *want* to help you. If you've been suffering from illness, a chronic medical condition, an injury that just won't heal, or even mental and emotional exhaustion, this ritual is one that allows you to open yourself up to the badass healing powers of your family tree.

Keep in mind that any healing ritual, ancestral or not, should not be used as a substitute for proper medical care—get thee to a trained health-care professional *in addition* to performing healing rituals.

To do this ritual, it's important to indulge in a bit of self-care. After all, wellness includes feeling healthy and clean in mind, body, and spirit. Start by running yourself a bath at whatever temperature you prefer. Add to your bathwater healing herbs like chamomile, ginseng, echinacea, or feverfew. The best way to do this is to add the fresh or dried herbs into a cloth sachet and place it in the water. If herbs and flowers are left to float about loose, you'll be picking soggy pieces of chamomile out of your deepest nooks and crannies for a while after your bath.

Light a white candle, place it beside the tub, and climb into your bath. As you soak, close your eyes and imagine your ancestors gently surrounding you with healing energy, enveloping you like you're covered in a warm, comforting blanket of love. Whether they're wrapping you in one of Grandma Sadie's frontier quilts, the bright sari cloth of your grandfather's home country, or the silk parachute that a great-uncle smuggled home after a war overseas, picture them encircling you with the warmth of generations of love and well-being.

Call your people as you immerse yourself in the bath, and say, *I call upon you, my people, my kith and kin, in a time of need. I ask your assistance and blessing, and that you bring me health and wellness. I am ill and uneasy, anxious and unwell, and I need your healing light. I ask you to watch over me, giving me the strength to heal. Keep me safe from further illness, and make me healthy and whole, body and soul. I ask you, my ancestors, to heal me in this time of sickness.*

Once the bathwater has cooled, it is time to move to your altar. Bring your white candle with you and place it in the center. Use it to light your favorite incense blend, and as the smoke begins to rise, envision your illness wafting away with the smoke. Again, speak to your people: *Ancestors, I ask you to take away my illness, carrying it out to the four winds, never to return. On the winds of the north, send this illness away, and in return bring me health. On the winds of the east, send this illness away, and in return bring me strength. On the winds of the south, send this illness away, and in return bring me vitality. On the winds of the west, send this illness away, and in return bring me life. Carry disease and pain, suffering and fear, so that they will go far away from me, scattering, and troubling me no more.*

Finally, it's time to make an offering of thanks. Your offering can be something small and simple—flowers you've picked, a glass of wine—or it can be more complex, like a painting you created or a piece of jewelry you made yourself. Place it on the altar, beside your white candle, so that all of your ancestors can see what you've brought them. Say, *Hail to you, my powerful people, I pay you tribute. I honor you and ask this one small gift. May your healing light and strength wash over me, bringing me wellness in this time of great need. Guide me and heal me, and ease my suffering.*

Take a few moments to meditate on what you will do when you're feeling better. How will you honor your people after you're no longer ill or anxious? Once you have finished, allow the candle to burn out on its own if possible. Leave the offering in place for seven days before disposing of it.

Power Ritual with Your Badass Kin

When we honor our ancestors, no matter how many generations we go back, it is mutually beneficial for both us and them. After all, who is as vested in our success and well-being as our family? If one of us accomplishes something great, it reflects positively on everyone in the bloodline, creating a shared and valuable legacy.

This power ritual calls upon both your maternal line and your paternal ancestors, separately, so you'll want to have a written list of names to call out as you're doing this working. Obviously, if you only want to work with one side of the family—for instance, your mother's people were full of drama and trauma and you're not ready to work with them—then simply skip over the line you wish to avoid.

Perform this ritual at your ancestor altar with an offering ready to present, but don't put it on the altar just yet. If you typically cast a circle or smudge a sacred space before ritual, do so. Put your favorite incense blend on your altar along with a glass of wine or water. Finally, place a tealight or votive candles on the altar to represent the various family members you're about to name—count them out ahead of time—as well as a large candle in the center. Take a few minutes to ground yourself, centering, and focusing on calling your ancestors to you. When you are ready, light your incense and the large candle, and place your offering on the altar, and call your people:

Ancestors, kin of my kin, blood of my blood, my people! I call out to you and invite you to join me in this sacred space, this place between my world and yours. I present these offerings, of fire, wine (or water), and bread, that you may always see in the darkness, that you may never thirst, that you may never hunger. Today, I call to you and welcome your strength, your power, your will, and your guidance.

Start by calling in your matrilineal line, beginning with the first deceased woman in your mother's ancestry. If your mother or grandmother is still living, don't include her. Begin by calling your people out by their full maiden names, and as you welcome each one, light the tealight that represents her. Invite at least three generations to join you, if you know their names, but try not to get too crazy—it will take you forever to call upon thirty or forty generations. Try to keep it to fewer than ten if possible.

I call now upon my mother's mother's line. I welcome my grandmother, Margaret Chapman, and her mother, Emily Weiss, and her mother, Caroline Emily Dieter, and her mother, Caroline Charlotte Grossberg, and her mother ... etc.

All women, mothers and grandmothers and great-grandmothers, all whose blood runs through mine. All women, mothers and grandmothers and great-grandmothers, all who raised the next generation of female power in my family. All women, mothers and grandmothers and great-grandmothers, who are daughters themselves. Come to this altar and accept my offerings.

Come to this altar, and share with me your strength, your power, your energy, your drive, your ambition, your will. Come to this altar, and accept my gratitude and love, mothers of my mother.

Next, call upon your patrilineal line. Again, light a candle for each individual you name, and try to keep the list of badass men in your direct line down to between three and ten generations. Remember, start with the most recently deceased generation. If that's your father, begin with him.

I call now upon my father's father's line. I welcome my father, Jackson Cole, and his father, Edward Cole, and his father, Albert Koehle, and his father, Karl Albert Koehlevesky, and his father ... and so on.

All men, fathers and grandfathers and great-grandfathers, all whose blood runs through mine. All men, fathers and grandfathers and great-grandfathers, all who raised the next generation of male power in my family. All men, fathers and grandfathers and great-grandfathers, who are sons themselves.

Come to this altar and accept my offerings. Come to this altar, and share with me your strength, your power, your energy, your drive, your ambition, your will. Come to this altar, and accept my love and gratitude, fathers of my father.

Finally, call upon the extended family. This will include people not in your direct matrilineal or paternal line of ancestry, but everyone connected to you via blood or marriage or adoption.

I call now upon my extended family, my beloved dead, my ancestors of the blood and the heart. I call now upon aunts and uncles, cousins and kin, all you relatives with whom I share spirit.

Come to this altar and accept my offerings. Come to this altar, and share with me your strength, your power, your energy, your drive, your ambition, your will. Come to this altar, and accept my gratitude and love, people of my people.

Spend as much time as you like calling out to your ancestors, drawing upon their strength and energy. Work with them, speak to them, and most importantly, *listen* to them. What are they telling you? What power can you gain from them? What success and accomplishment will they push you towards?

When you are ready, conclude your ritual by thanking your people.

Ancestors, kin of my kin, blood of my blood, my people! I call out to you and thank you for joining me in this sacred space, this place between my world and yours. Thank you to my mother's mothers, to my father's fathers, and all the relatives who have shared their strength with me. I ask that you continue to aid me in my endeavors, and I thank you for blessing me with your strength, your power, your will, and your guidance.

Extinguish the candle and leave the offerings on your altar for twenty-four hours before disposing of them.

Silent Supper with the Ancestors

In many modern magical traditions, especially among those of us who do spirit work, a silent supper is a great way to connect with those who came before us. You may have heard this referred to as a *dumb supper*, which originates from the Old English terminology in which the word *dumb* was used as a synonym for *mute*.

Today, holding a silent supper is a wonderful ritual that can be done with the entire family to honor your ancestors, but it does require some pre-planning if a group of people will be present. Although these are often held at Samhain, the time when the veil between our world and the spirit realm is thinning, you can have a silent supper any time of the year. Ultimately, there is no one right or wrong way to have a silent supper; the best way to do it is the way that works best for your family and your needs.

Set your dining table with a fancy cloth, white or black; if you've got black or white dishware, bring that out too. Do you have access to black cutlery? This is the time to get it out of the box in the cupboard. Add fresh flowers in vases, and some candles—again, use black or white if possible. Make your table look as special as you can. Imagine your grandmother walking in, looking around, and saying, *Oh, I like what you've done with the place, dear.*

Be sure to make your dining area sacred, either by casting a circle (if that's part of your normal tradition), smudging, asperging, or some other method. Turn off phones and televisions, eliminating outside distractions.

Your menu choices are up to you but try to focus on foods that would fit into an ancestral menu—there are several recipes in chapter 10 to get you started. You can also make traditional soul cakes, which are baked for the spirits of the dead in many European countries. Use seasonally appropriate foods, serving dishes with apples, late fall vegetables, and game if it's fall, or light greens, eggs, and dairy items for spring.

Set a place at your table for each guest you've invited; use place cards to avoid confusion regarding who gets to sit where. The spot at the head of the table should be reserved for the place of the ancestors. Although it's nice to have a place setting for every single person in your family you wish to honor, that can be impractical; instead, use a single candle at the ancestor seat to represent the ancestral collective. Shroud the ancestor chair in black or white cloth. Give them a plate, a cup, knives and forks, and a napkin, just like all of the other place settings. After all, this is their meal.

Remember that this is a noiseless occasion, not a carnival; if you or your guests have younger children who might become restless when they have to stay quiet, you may wish to leave them out of the silent supper. Ask each adult guest to bring a note to the dinner. The note's contents will be kept private and should contain messages they want to pass along to the ancestors.

When hosting a silent supper, the idea (obviously) is that no one can speak, which can make a host's job tricky. You'll be responsible for anticipating each guest's needs without them communicating verbally to you. Depending on the size of your table, make sure each end has its own salt and pepper shakers, butter, water pitchers, and so on. Also, watch your guests carefully to see if anyone needs a fresh napkin, a drink refill, or an extra fork to replace the one they just dropped on the floor.

No one should speak from the time they enter the dining area. Instruct your guests in advance that as they enter the room, they should take a moment to stop at the ancestor chair to offer a silent prayer to the dead. Once everyone has been seated, join hands, and take a moment to silently bless the meal and thank the ancestors for joining you. As the host or hostess, seat yourself directly across from the ancestor chair, and serve the meal by passing each dish around the table clockwise to your guests. Be sure to put someone responsible beside the ancestor chair; that individual is in charge of putting food on the ancestor plate. No one should eat until all guests—including the ancestors—have been served.

When everyone has finished their meal, each guest should get out the note they brought for the ancestors. Approach the head of the table where the ancestors sit, focus on the note, and then burn it in the candle's flame—have a plate or small cauldron on hand to catch burning bits of paper—and then quietly return to your seat. Your guests, again moving in a clockwise direction, should each follow suit, one at a time. When everyone has had their turn, join hands once again, and offer a silent farewell prayer to the ancestors, bidding them a safe journey and thanking them for their company.

Everyone should leave the room in silence. Stop at the ancestor chair on your way out of the room and say goodbye one more time. After your guests have gone for the night, place the ancestor plate on your altar, and leave it there for twenty-four hours before disposing of it.

Simple Prayer for Guidance

Are you stuck finding the solution to a problem? Have you asked all of your friends for input but nothing quite seems to work for you or even make sense? This is when it's time to reach out to your ancestral tribe and ask your people for their guidance. After all, they've seen a lot more than you have, so why haven't you asked them for advice? This is a simple prayer you can do when you're sitting at your altar, and you need some insight from your badass kinfolk. It's a lot less reverent than some people might prefer and is pretty straightforward, but if your kin are the kind of people who appreciate that sort of thing, give it a shot. If not, modify it to make it more formal, as needed.

> *I call my people, all of you!*
> *I need to know, what should I do?*
> *Guide me, steer me, offer advice,*
> *A solution to my problem would be nice.*
> *Share your wisdom, share your insight,*
> *Help me choose what's most right.*
> *Grandfathers and grandmothers,*
> *Uncles, aunts, sisters, brothers,*
> *I call my people, all of you!*
> *I need to know, show me what to do.*

Six

PROBLEM ANCESTORS — YOU CAN'T CHOOSE YOUR PEOPLE

At some point in your research, you're going to uncover some problem ancestors, or the people in your family, whether by blood or marriage or adoption, who did horrific things. This is quite possibly one of the hardest parts of ancestor work to deal with, because while we'd like to believe our people were all noble and grand, here's a plot twist for you: they weren't. In fact, some of our ancestors downright sucked. They weren't badasses, they were terrible people who did terrible things to other people.

Obviously, you're the only one who can decide what sort of behavior in your family tree you can live with and what you find unpleasant. But let's talk about a few examples of things you might have to contend with the further back you go in time.

For about four to six generations during the seventeenth and eighteenth centuries, one branch of my direct ancestors owned other people. That's my elephant in the room when looking at my ancestors, and I struggle with it on the regular. And don't get me wrong—all of those people in those four to six generations were wealthy enough to own hundreds, or possibly thousands of acres of land in colonial Virginia. They'd be perfect to call upon for assistance with financial matters ... but I don't. I can't bring myself to ask for financial assistance from people who built their own fortunes on the backs of enslaved people. I've seen the documentation, the itemized wills and testaments in which property is enumerated as *Four hundred acres on the banks of the Guinea Creek, two good tables, five chickens, and one adult male Negro.*

I just can't do it. I've got plenty of other people in my tree I can call upon for wealth and prosperity; I won't engage with the people in those few generations for this matter. That's my own standard. Yours may be different, but that's mine.

If one of your ancestors caused direct harm to another, that can be problematic as well. You'll want to make sure you don't call them both to join you at the same time. Did you have an ancestor who was responsible for the death of another? I did. Imagine having these two people seated across from each other at the family Thanksgiving dinner, because that's exactly what it would be like if I were to invite them both to my altar and ritual space. It would be uncomfortable and painful for both of them.

Maybe someone existed in your lifetime—or close to it—who perpetuated a cycle of abuse upon either you or your parents. This can be tricky to navigate—and again, you're the only one who can decide how you want to deal with these particularly unpleasant branches of your family tree.

You don't have to like them. You don't have to work with them. You're under no obligation to have anything to do with them if they've done things that make you uncomfortable. But consider this, for just a moment.

There are times when ancestors who have done appalling, horrific things might just come in handy. There are times when we need protection or guardianship, and circumstances in which we are about to take on major conflict and need power and strength. Can you find a way to draw boundaries between your existing spiritual needs and the heinous acts your person has committed?

One of my problem people is Thomas Jefferson. While not in my direct line of ancestry, he is distantly connected through a tangle of marriage, blood, and other degrees of separation. Jefferson owned human beings as property, and forced at least one—his wife's half-sister—to bear his children, beginning while she was still a young teen, among some other repulsive acts. He also was one of our founding fathers, a statesman, a diplomat, and the third president of the United States and primary author of the Declaration of Independence. So, do I work with Jefferson on an ancestral level? I'd be hard pressed to do so—I've got plenty of other options—but if I was about to write a political manifesto declaring my independence from an oppressive and tyrannical government… well, he *might* turn out to be useful, despite all of the other despicable things he did. I'm not prepared to work with Jefferson yet, by any stretch of the imagination. If I ever do, I'll have to lay down boundaries that let him know in no uncertain terms, that the vile actions he engaged in were and are intolerable. He may find this boundary unacceptable and refuse to work with me—and I can live with that. I'm truly not sure I'll ever be able to bring myself to call upon him.

Maybe you've got an ancestor who was a war hero but you're having trouble justifying your work with him because in addition to saving an entire platoon from slaughter, he was responsible for the deaths of dozens of other people, civilians and soldiers alike. Which do you focus on? Only you can decide for sure, but if you're ever in a position where you need to call upon your kin for courage in a frightening situation, this ancestor might be the one to reach out to, warts and all.

Meanwhile, as you're trying to figure out what to do with problematic kinfolk, you can set them on the back burner for a while. You've got plenty of other badass people you can work with, at least until you're ready to tackle unsavory Great-Grandpa Whoever. Let him stew a bit, unbothered.

How do you leave these problem ancestors out of your workings? You specifically make sure you don't invite them in. Think of your ancestor altar as a representation of your family home. Who do you invite into your house as guests? People you know and like, sure. You probably also welcome people that you maybe don't know well, but you'd like to get to know better. Know who you *don't* have to invite in to sit on your couch and put their feet up on your coffee table? People that are abusive jerks.

Same goes for your ancestor altar, and your practice as a whole. You're allowed to leave those people out. Doing so is easier than you think; refuse to acknowledge them on your altar until you're prepared to deal with them. Don't include any photographs, cremains, heirlooms, or anything associated with that person—or persons—on your ancestor altar. When you do rituals calling upon your people, skip over that one's name. Don't call out an invocation to *All of my people* if what you really mean is *All of my people except those three cousins who were high-ranking officers in Germany's Nazi party.*

Can they try to push their way in? Sure. Just like at a family reunion when that one racist, abusive uncle shows up drunk and things get really uncomfortable because no one knows what to do with him ... until a cousin firmly tells him *No*, as she escorts him to his car. You get to tell these people *No* if they show up unrequested, unwanted, and uninvited. The word *No* is a complete sentence, and it's an empowering act of badassery to use it. No one is entitled to make you feel bad in your own house. Kick them to the curb as needed, with no regrets.

It's a good idea to take work with these ancestors slowly at first. You'll still be feeling each other out, and if the person is someone who caused pain to you or other loved ones while they were alive, you're going to have to find some middle ground. You don't necessarily have to forgive them their trespasses, so to speak, but you may be able to someday reach a point of agreeing to be civil to one another.

Don't be afraid to ask other ancestral guides to run interference for you. Was grandpa a raging alcoholic who liked to terrorize his neighbors? Call in that spunky aunt who always stood up to him, and ask her to be a gatekeeper, watching over his behavior in the afterlife and in your space.

When you finally decide to let your problem ancestors into your sacred space, lay out the ground rules and expectations. You can say things like *I welcome you to my altar, but boundaries will be respected, no pain shall be tolerated, no hurt will be allowed. I welcome you to my altar, for as long as you are willing and able to treat me with the honor and respect I deserve. I welcome you to my altar, a space that is for love and healing, and have no room or time for those who would cause me suffering.*

You can also tell them *why* you're laying those ground rules. Make it very clear which past behaviors caused the disconnect between you and the individual—they most likely already know, but it can be empowering to verbalize it. Let them know: *Your alcoholism caused fear for my brothers and me, when you abandoned me it made me distrustful of others and has cost me relationships, the abuse you perpetuated on my mother created physical and emotional scars.*

If your problem ancestor was someone who died before you were born, you can still take the same approach. Tell them why you've been reluctant to work with them and lay out the rules for interaction. As long as they're willing to coexist peacefully with you, and you're willing to stick to your guns as to what you'll put up with and what you won't, it's possible that you can heal some of the damage that was done in the past.

Ritual to Banish a Problem Ancestor

If you've got an ancestor who keeps popping in and you just can't get them to take No for an answer, it might be time to tackle a banishing ritual. This is an aggressive and powerful method to completely get rid of someone, but if you have a person who caused harm to you or others, at some point you may feel like it's your only option. Keep in mind that if you do this ritual effectively, the target is gone for good—if there's any chance you'll want to work with them again in the future, this might not be the best approach. Ultimately, banishing is in itself an act of badassery, because it's a way to reclaim our power, our space, and our sense of self.

To do this ritual, you'll need to remove the photos of everyone else on your ancestor altar that you do work with and replace them with a single unframed photo of the person you want to banish. They should be the only one whose image is in your space right now. If you don't have a photograph of the individual, you can use vital records documentation—a birth or death certificate—or even a paper doll that you've written the person's name on. You'll also need a black candle—in many modern magical traditions, black is the color associated with banishing magic—and a cast iron cauldron or other fire-safe bowl.

Light the black candle and close your eyes. Imagine yourself standing on one end of a long bridge, suspended over a deep chasm. On the other end of the bridge is the person you wish to banish, facing you. What do you want to tell them? Do you want them to know why you're sending them away? Can you tell them how much damage they've caused? *Great grandfather, I am banishing you, exiling you from my life and my heart for the pain you have inflicted. I am eliminating you from my future and am taking back any power you've had over me.* Although you don't have to speak aloud, you may find it empowering to do so. Sometimes a loud and angry voice sends a message; yell your words across the bridge to get your point across if it feels right.

Take the photo and begin burning the paper around the edges using the flame from the black candle. As you do so, let the ancestor know that you are burning away your familial connections to them. *I burn away my feelings towards you. I burn away any animosity, jealousy, sense of hurt that I have towards you. I burn away my ties to you, and your ties to me. I burn away all of our connections, I burn away our links, I cut every cord that ever existed between us.*

Now, imagine yourself dropping that burning photo onto the bridge. Feel the flames as the bridge catches fire. Encourage it, send it forward, so that every plank on the bridge is soon consumed by fire. Burn as much of the paper as you can, little by little, before you drop it into the bowl. Visualize the bridge engulfed and ablaze, and ultimately collapsing into the chasm. Now there is nothing left but a vast gap between you and the person who caused so much pain. They'll never be able to reach you again—that giant canyon, spanning many generations, will keep them far away from you and from your future descendants.

Look at them one last time. Do you have anything else you need to say? Because this is your last chance. Get it out of your system. As the photo turns to ash, shout across the chasm, *I banish you from my life, I banish you from my home, I banish you from my world.*

Extinguish the black candle and take it, along with the ashes of the photo you just burned, to a place far away from your home. Dig a hole and bury them, scatter them to the winds, or drop them in a moving body of water to be carried off and out of your life. Once you've done this, return home without looking back, cleanse your altar thoroughly, and reset it with the badass ancestors who love you.

Transgenerational Trauma Healing

There's a concept that trauma is passed down from one generation to the next, and that each subsequent generation, although further and further removed from the original cause of pain, still suffers from it as much as their ancestors did. In the United States, we're really good at ancestral trauma; forced immigration, religious oppression, and unwanted displacement were widespread for a significant part of our history, and people are still experiencing its aftereffects today. Even immigrants who came to the U.S. voluntarily still left their family and friends in their homelands; if you came to the New World to settle, it was understood that you'd probably never again see those who were left behind. All of these events led to a disconnect in which we lost many of our ancestral customs.

African men, women, and children were violently uprooted from their homes and forced into the trans-Atlantic slave trade. Native Americans were exterminated or pushed further west, all in the interest of manifest destiny. Hundreds of thousands of Jews fled their homes in Europe to escape the Holocaust, and during the same period, Japanese Americans were interned in camps here in the states. Is it any wonder that people today are still trying to heal from collective transgenerational damage? Working with your ancestors directly to mend this disconnect is beneficial not just to you, but to them … and also to the many generations yet to come. Can you find a way to release your ancestors from the burdens of the trauma they experienced during their lifetimes?

One way to do this is with a ritual to help them move forward. To be clear, this is not a case of telling Great-Great-Aunt Pernilla that she just needs to get over it and move on. What this *can* do is let your people know that you feel their pain, understand it, and you want to help them triumph over it.

Trauma Healing Ritual

Prior to beginning this working, it's a good idea to get yourself into the right head space—working with ancestral trauma can be draining, and you don't want to do it when you're tired, depressed, or feeling off-kilter. Make sure you're well rested before you begin; you may even want to take a ritual bath and eat a nourishing meal to prepare your body, mind, and spirit. Be sure your altar is clean and purified before you begin.

For this ritual, you'll need a blue candle, as the color blue is associated with healing. Place it on your altar and light it. When you're ready to begin, call your ancestors in one at a time or in groups. If you're trying to heal a specific transgenerational trauma and know when it took place, you can simply call in the generation that directly experienced it and all of their subsequent descendants. If you're working with something more general, concentrate on the family line that seems to be the most directly impacted.

As you invite your people in, close your eyes and feel their presence around you. Welcome them in, saying *Thank you, my ancestors, my mothers and fathers, for joining me this evening. Welcome to my altar, and know you are safe with me. My home is your home as well.*

Once you have welcomed them in, it's time to encourage them to reclaim the power that was taken from them by trauma all of those years ago. If you know the source of the trauma, call it out, as you take back power on your ancestors' behalf. As you do so, you can chant or sing your words, or yell them out like a battle cry. Move or dance or stomp your feet if it feels right. Your invocation might go something like this:

> My people, my clan, my tribe, my circle,
> You have been broken and beaten,
> you have been harmed and hurt,
> Abused and shamed, robbed and
> marginalized, oppressed and subjugated.
> That ends tonight, and healing begins.
> My people, my clan, my tribe, my circle,
> I reclaim your power for you, taking it
> back from those who would crush us,
> From those who took your land,
> who violated your bodies,
> And stole our heritage.
> My people, my clan, my tribe, my circle,
> I reclaim your strength for you, building
> you up, making you whole once more,
> Growing in perfection and power and energy,
> Retrieving that which is rightfully ours.
> My people, my clan, my tribe, my circle,
> Together we fight, together we rise, together we stand,
> Together we release and together we heal.
> Because we are many, and we are powerful, as one family.

Continue your invocation until you feel you have said all you need to say. When you are done, take some time to meditate on your ancestors, and the gifts of healing you can give one another. Before you end your ritual, closely pull as many of them to yourself as you can so that you can take strength from one another's power. Imagine them surrounding you, touching you, holding each other, and forming a tight circle with their love. Call them out by name if you can.

I draw Great-Grandma Charlotte to me, I draw Great Aunt Zariah to me, I draw Cousin Marlowe to me, I draw all of my mother's people, going back nine generations, to me …

When you have called them all, think about this incredible network of powerful people in your ancestral line. Build the energy, and chant, *Blood of my blood, hearts of my heart, souls of my soul, we are happy, we are healing, we are whole.* Repeat your chant as many times as needed and feel the magic and power of your ancestral connections surrounding you.

When you're ready to end the ritual, bid your people farewell. You can simply say, *Thank you for joining me, and for healing with me, and working with me this night,* or say something with more detail or complexity. Say what's in your heart when you let them go.

After your ancestral guides have gone, take a moment to reflect on the healing process. Think about how your life could change as you begin the steps to battle transgenerational trauma. When finished, extinguish the candle.

Seven

BADASS ANCESTORS OF THE HEART

Our ancestors of the heart are those individuals who were real people in our lives but were not necessarily genetically related to us. Sometimes they're adopted family members, and just as often they are people who have come into our world and made such an impact on our lives that even after death, they still have messages of wisdom and power to share with us. If you don't have familial ancestors to call upon, and you're not crazy about calling in badass archetypes, you can still work with your heart ancestors in a respectful and loving way.

Working with spiritual or heart ancestors is even more rewarding than working with familial guides, because ancestors of the heart are people you *chose*, and who chose you in return. Unlike biological ancestors, with whom you're kind of stuck with the luck of the draw, and archetypal ancestors, who have their own flaws and foibles, a spirit ancestor is one that you can work with and often feel unconditional love. Keep in mind that there can be overlap between those who are ancestors of the heart, and those who are spiritual kinfolk.

Ancestors of the Heart

Your heart ancestors are the people you've chosen, for whatever reason, to love—and you've allowed them to love you in return. They're the ones who stick by us even when our so-called "real family" can't be bothered to offer their support. Our ancestors of the heart can include dear friends who have passed beyond the veil, foster parents, neighbors, or even schoolteachers. If they are someone who loved you, and you loved them back, and they had an influence upon your life, count them as a heart ancestor.

If you're working with ancestors of the heart, be sure to ask permission before calling them in. In particular, if you're part of a majority ethnic or cultural group and want to work with heart ancestors from a culture or ethnicity that has been traditionally oppressed, don't simply claim them as your own. Show the respect they're due and ask them if it's okay for you to work with them. Claiming people who don't belong to you, simply because you've decided to work with them, can be a bad idea.

That's not to say that guides from cultures other than your own can't or won't appear to you; they can and will do so if the mood strikes them. If that happens, work with them as much as they allow, but do so respectfully—don't claim ownership of marginalized ancestors.

Ritual to Honor Heart Ancestors

When it's time to honor your heart ancestors, it's important to make it special. You get to call them in just like you do your badass kinfolk. Set up your altar with candles and photos, and include some fresh home-baked bread, a goblet of wine or consecrated water, and a fresh apple or other fruit. Light your candles—one for each heart ancestor—and light your favorite incense. Take a moment to breathe, grounding yourself, and ask them to come knock upon your door: *My people, my friends, those who live in my heart, I call you forth and ask that you come to my door.*

Visualize yourself opening a door and seeing your heart ancestors standing in front of it. Invite them in: *My people, my friends, those who live in my heart, I welcome you to my home, and my world, where you always have a seat at my table. We may not be blood kin, but you are always in my heart.* Imagine them walking through your door and surrounding you at the altar.

Raise the goblet of wine and ask your heart ancestors to share it with you. *My people, my friends, those who live in my heart, you nurtured me and cared for me. You showed me love unconditionally and you accepted me. You supported me and celebrated with me. You held me when I wept, lifted me up when I fell, and showed me how strong I could be, even once you were gone, and I offer you this wine in tribute.* Visualize your people passing the wine, each of them taking a sip, and say, *May you never thirst in the afterlife.*

Raise the bread and offer it to your heart ancestors: *My people, my friends, those who live in my heart, you gave me abundance when I had nothing, you shared your meals with me when I was hungry, you offered me hospitality when I had nowhere to go. You bestowed blessings upon me even when I didn't know I needed them, and I offer you this bread in tribute.* Picture your heart ancestors each taking a bite of the bread, and say, *May you never hunger in the afterlife.*

Finally, take the apple and raise it in honor of your people: *My people, my friends, those who live in my heart, you inspired me when I had nothing to look towards, you pushed me when I faltered, you gave me courage when I needed it the most. Your wisdom and kindness helped shape the person I have become, and I offer you this apple in tribute.* Can you see your people passing the apple around, each of them taking a bite? Tell them *May you never want in the afterlife.*

Close your eyes and visualize all of your people, surrounding you, enjoying your hospitality and feeling welcome in your life. Is there a particular one you'd like to thank for something special? Now is the time to do so. You can say things like:

- Mrs. Knepper, thank you for watching out for me in seventh grade when that mean Becky in your class bullied me.
- Mr. Billy, thank you for teaching me how to fish the summer I stayed with my grandpa.
- Kumiko, thank you for showing me the beauty found in art, and for letting me know my skills have value.

After you have thanked them, take a moment to consider how you can live in a way that will make them proud. When you're ready, it's time to tell them farewell. Imagine yourself opening the door once more: *My people, my friends, those who live in my heart, it is time for us to say goodbye for now. I thank you for your visit, and you will always be welcome in my home, as you are in my heart.* See them walking through the door, and as they leave, know that you'll see them again soon.

Leave your offerings on the altar for twenty-four hours before disposing of them.

Spiritual Ancestors

Once we recognize that who we are isn't just about biology or strands on a DNA chain, but also about ideas and thoughts, we can start working with our spiritual ancestors. Our spiritual kinfolk are the ones who have directly shaped our thoughts, beliefs, and ideas to help frame the person we have become. They can be priests or pastors who guided us during times of spiritual crisis, shamanic practitioners, ascended masters, or even the high priestess who first introduced you to your spiritual journey. Even prophets or holy figures such as the Buddha or Jesus, could be spiritual ancestors as long as they are people whose teachings have colored your spiritual belief system.

Ritual to Honor Spiritual Ancestors

Our spiritual ancestors want us to continue their traditions. They hope that the lessons imparted on us will be carried forward. In thanking them for their wisdom and philosophies, we let them know that their efforts weren't wasted. For this ritual, decorate your altar with three candles in colors that speak to you, as well as a pot of live flowers. Light your incense, and say *My spiritual ancestors, I have received your wisdom and I am grateful for it. I send an offering of thanks to you, rising upon this smoke and across the veil to you.*

Light your first candle, and say *I am filled with light and love and spiritual growth because of you, and I thank you.* When you light the second candle, say *I am filled with wisdom and knowledge and a sense of purpose because of you, and I thank you.* Finally, light the third candle, saying *I am spiritually whole and healthy, and will share the bounty of your favors with those who need it, for the greater good, and I thank you.*

Take the flowers in your hands, and inhale deeply. Take in their fresh, heady scent. Close your eyes, and say *My spiritual ancestors, may I always hear your voice when you speak to me. May I always call you when I know you are listening. May I always find courage in the darkness when you provide me with light. May I always move forward from pain when you send me healing. May I always feel enlightened when you guide me with your wisdom. May I always find my true calling when you send me a test. May I always feel reborn and renewed, when you send me hope and inspiration. My spiritual ancestors, I thank you for your gifts.*

Extinguish the candles and repeat this petition for three consecutive nights. After the third night, take the pot of flowers and place them in a sunny spot; each time you water them, remember the gifts that your spiritual kinfolk have bestowed upon you.

Ritual to Honor the Forgotten Dead

Those of us who follow the various magical belief systems are pretty good about honoring our dead. If you're doing ancestor work, you're probably better at it than most people. However, there's one group that often gets overlooked; if you want to include them in your rituals, it's perfectly okay to do so. They may or may not be related to you, but sometimes calling them in and simply honoring them can be of benefit to you. These are the people we consider the Forgotten Dead, the ones who died somewhere alone or unwanted or unloved, with no one to mourn them or sing their names with honor as they crossed through the veil. They're the people who vanish from the records and end up in a transient camp somewhere. They're the ones buried with no headstone because no one cared enough or could afford to pay for a marker. They're the ones who died in nursing homes, under bridges, or in remote fields somewhere, with no one to even remember who they were.

They're the men, women, and children who have crossed over and whose spirits are lost to memory. However, by speaking for them and giving them a voice, you can not only empower them, but also open things up so that if they want to thank you, you might just benefit from their gratitude.

You will need white candles for this ritual, one each to represent a group of forgotten people, whether it's men, women, children, people from a certain geographic area, victims of crime, and so on; group people in any way that works for you. If there's someone specific you know of that died alone, you can designate a single candle to represent that person as well. Do this ritual at your ancestor altar. Light your incense, but don't light the candles just yet.

Take a moment to reflect on what your ancestors have left you as well as the memories and stories you have of them. Think about what memories and stories you'll leave behind for your descendants when you're gone. Now imagine how it would feel if no one was left to mourn you. Think about the idea that future generations might have nothing left to remember you by. It's a pretty sobering thought, isn't it? That's why it can be healing to call forth the forgotten dead. Just because you don't want to call any random dangerous beings into your life, be sure to include a petition to your ancestors to watch over you and protect you as you work with the forgotten—you only want benevolent beings to come join you at your altar:

I am blessed by my memories of my ancestors, thankful that I remember the stories of my dead, of those who have fallen and crossed over the veil from this world to the next. I ask my known and unknown people to watch over me, protecting me from harm or danger, as I honor another group, the forgotten dead. Tonight, I honor them and pay tribute. Tonight, I remember those who were forgotten. Tonight, I memorialize you, the unknown, the unloved, the unwanted of our world. Whoever you may have been in life, tonight, now, in death, you are mine as you watch from the other side, and I honor you, if you may be called benevolent and kind.

Light the first of your candles—let's assume it's assigned to the forgotten women: *Women who were lost to us, how did you pass? Were you old and alone, crossing over with no one but your own ghosts to keep you company? Were you young and healthy, taken from us unexpectedly, your crossing as much a surprise to you as to anyone else? Forgotten women, those who shine a light in the darkness, your spirits are with me. I remember you and want you to know you are honored. You are remembered.*

Light the next candle, and call the forgotten men: *Men who were lost to us, how did you pass? Did you die in a strange place, far from family and friends? Were you in your prime, taken away too soon, and unexpectedly? Forgotten men, those who shine a light in the darkness, your spirits are with me. I remember you and want you to know you are honored. You are remembered.*

Work your way through whatever groups you have chosen to call; light a candle for each one and make sure they know they are honored and remembered. When you have lit all your candles, say *All of you, those unknown, you may have left this world unnoticed, but for now, you are unforgotten. I remember you. Know that you are with me in memory and in spirit. If you are kind and benevolent, we may someday speak again.*

Extinguish the candles and say *I have honored you and now you must move on. Go back to the places from which you came, go back knowing that you were remembered. Go back across the veil and remain in that world. Farewell, rest easy, and may the coming parts of your journey be worthy of you. Hail the traveler.*

When you know they have left, purify and cleanse your altar space in the way that you see fit.

Eight
CONNECTING TO ARCHETYPAL BADASSES

Archetypes appear in nearly every cultural context. If there's no ancestor to work for us with a particular issue we're facing, what about strong people from history and mythology? Consider working with names from your genetic heritage, even if they're not biologically related to you. You can work with historical figures such as French martyr Jeanne d'Arc, Scottish freedom fighter William Wallace, or African American activist Martin Luther King. Perhaps you only want to work with a symbolic archetype like that of the warrior, the rebel, or the sage—or even mythological and legendary figures like Robin Hood, Baba Yaga, or Morgan Le Fay.

When you have made the decision to not work with your biological ancestors, there is always the option of working with cultural archetypes. Carl Jung, the well-known psychologist, used a system of archetypes to describe images that relate to the collective unconsciousness. As far as Jung is concerned, every culture or belief system has a series of common archetypes that every single person can relate to. These archetypal figures appear across cultures and societies throughout the history of time. In addition to serving as cultural symbols, archetypes also represent behavioral patterns that define our personalities.

The search for meaning in our natural world is the central driving force of spirituality. The shared human mindset creates archetypes as a way of rationalizing the things we seek to understand. In other words, we create archetypes as part of the collective unconscious, as symbolic images that everyone understands, no matter where or when they live.

One of the wonderful things about working with archetypes is that in addition to being relatable for people of nearly any culture around the world, Jung believed that archetypes formed the foundation of religious belief, so once you figure out which ones to work with, tying them into your spirituality makes a lot more sense. As part of the human search for wholeness, Jung believed that we—that's the societal *we*, not the individuals you and me—create archetypes as a form of pattern-building.

How would you call figures like Merlin or Baba Yaga into your life as badass ancestral guides? After all, how can we have any right to claim them when they didn't exist anywhere but in mythology? Consider for a moment that throughout history, people have worked spiritually with figures and beings who are biologically unrelated to them. Gods, earth spirits, elementals, you name it—at some point, someone has called upon them. Working with archetypes is the same principle, but you'd simply invite them in as spiritual ancestors, rather than of your bloodline.

Let's break down some different archetypes into their different personas and explore some ways that you can work with them as chosen ancestral guides.

The Sage or Crone

Do you know someone who values ideas and wisdom more than they do material bounty? The sage or crone is a good listener and can help break down complicated ideas into a way that everyone can understand. They don't like to be perceived as ignorant and can sometimes struggle with decision making because they're always trying to weigh their options. Sages follow a constant desire to discover the truth—both in the world around them, and themselves—not to control or change it but to understand it. The sage or crone can be a benevolent mentor and source of great insight when you really need to delve deeper into a problem.

One of the greatest reasons to work with the sage, sometimes viewed as the *Elder*, or the *Senex*, in an archetypal and spiritual sense, is that this figure is driven by the desire to offer direction and guidance to those who ask for it; they've learned from their own mistakes and are willing to share. This makes the sage a perfect focal point when it comes to requests for advice from your ancestral guides.

For some examples of the sage, look to badass mythological figures. Characters like Merlin, for instance, from the Arthurian cycles of legend, are known for their wisdom and insight. The tales of Merlin and other wise old men and women lie at the heart of western culture. Although Merlin is often associated with magic, he's often called upon by Arthur for guidance and mentorship. He's the Obi-Wan Kenobi (or perhaps the Yoda) of Arthurian legend.

In Homer's *Iliad*, Nestor of Gerenia offers advice to Odysseus and his men; he encourages Achilles and Agamemnon to find a way to reconcile after years of conflict. His wise counsel is moderated by humor and a bit of boasting, and Homer describes him as a man of "sweet words." Even when his advice leads to disaster, Nestor has the best interests of his friends at heart.

Baba Yaga is a witch who appears in Russian and Slavic folklore. A seer and prophetess, she is also considered as a keeper of secret knowledge. She's full of things to share, but knowledge tends to

have a price; if you do any work at all with Baba Yaga, you'll probably find yourself sent off on a side quest before she decides to bless
you with her knowledge. Rest assured that if she does offer you
any guidance, you'll have earned it.

Plenty of real-life sages have lived throughout history; consider
working with people who were knowledgeable and shared information with others for the greater good. Not sure who to work
with? What about Benjamin Franklin, who was not only a diplomat and politician, but also a great inventor, philosopher, and poly-
math? Without Ben Franklin's wisdom, we wouldn't have bifocal
glasses or lightning rods. He started America's first lending library,
and laid the groundwork for the structure of the United States
postal system. Franklin invented numerous designs, but never pat-
ented any of them—he saw them as a gift to the American people.

Hildegard of Bingen, later canonized as Saint Hildegard, was
a twelfth-century German abbess. She was a composer of incredibly beautiful music, a philosopher, and a Christian mystic. She
wrote books on theology and even created her own language,
Lingua Ignota, which she used for spiritual writing. In addition to
experiencing visions—which Hildegard attributed to the light of
God—she developed an extensive scientific knowledge of botany
and herbal medicines, which she studied while tending the monastery gardens. She became skilled at the diagnosis and treatment of
ailments and injuries, especially the combination of physical treatment with the spiritual. Her holistic approach earned her great
respect as a wise healer.

The Seven Sages of the Bamboo Grove of third-century China
were a group of scholars and poets known for not only their wisdom but also their emphasis of free thought and individual expression. The Seven Sages, sometimes called the Seven Worthies, were
part of the Daoist movement. They found themselves fleeing pal-

ace life, because the criticism of the court that came along with art, music, and poetry was often ill-received. Interestingly enough, similarly named groups of scholars and philosophers existed in a number of cultures, including early India and ancient Greece.

Hypatia was a mathematician, philosopher, and astronomer who lived in Alexandria during the late fourth century. An academic with insatiable curiosity, she was a teacher at her city's university, and regularly performed scientific experiments, mapped out mathematical equations, and dedicated her life to learning. As a professor at the University of Alexandria, she would have had access to its Great Library, and was often found surrounded by eager scholars hoping to absorb some of her knowledge. Hypatia was killed by a Christian mob, who saw an educated and empowered woman as a threat to their faith, but she remained a symbol of the vast cultural and educational center that was Alexandria.

In addition to historical and folkloric sages and crones, you can even call upon symbolic figures like the wise hermit from the tarot, who represents guidance from within.

The Warrior

The warrior archetype is one of the most badass of all—and your definition of what makes a warrior may be different than other people's. Rest assured, the warrior is not always male; there are plenty of badass female warrior archetypes you can call upon for your work. As with all archetypes, there's a uniquely personal nature to doing spiritual work with the warrior. Who is a warrior? They're someone who fights for their ideals and beliefs, lives by a personal code of honor, and speaks out and defends those who have no voice of their own.

Why work with the warrior archetype? Well, for starters, it's great to invite warrior energy into your life when you're about to deal with situations of conflict. You can also call upon warriors for protection, to develop inner strength and fortitude, and when you need to be courageous in the face of battle. The warrior, who is often reluctant to step into combat haphazardly, is worth invoking when you need someone to have your back. The warrior exercises leadership, owns his or her mistakes, and makes informed decisions based on advice and counsel from trusted parties.

When it comes to folklore and legend, you've got plenty of options for warrior archetypes. Think in terms of people who are strong leaders. A strategic thinker behind the scenes can be just as powerful as a general in the field. Warrior archetypes in mythology could include Brunhild of the Valkyries, just for starters. This warrior princess from the Norse Eddas and the saga of the Volsungs was pretty badass. A powerful shieldmaiden, she killed the great fighter Sigurd the Dragon Slayer after he deceived her into marrying someone else. Having zero tolerance for bad behavior, Brunhild dispatched Sigurd for his betrayal.

Achilles appears in Greek mythology as the quintessential (although clearly flawed) warrior. During the Trojan War, Achilles established himself as a hero and one of the greatest fighters anyone had ever seen. He showed up in Troy with a massive fleet of fifty ships and more than two thousand Myrmidon soldiers; once he led them into battle, he demonstrated not only his physical strength but some excellent planning skills as well. Although Achilles fell in battle to an arrow striking his famously exposed heel, he remains an excellent example of the warrior mindset.

If you look at history, you've got a wealth of warriors to choose from. How about Scottish freedom fighters like William Wallace or Robert the Bruce, who lived eight centuries ago and were instrumental in Scotland's quest for independence? Or Jeanne d'Arc, the Maid of Orleans, burned as a heretic, but an enduring symbol of French nationalism and unity against oppression?

If your ancestry hails from one of the many African cultures, you have a rich tapestry of culture and history to choose from. The Dahomey Amazons, who hailed from what is now Benin, were total badasses. Although they began as an all-female hunting squad, they soon turned into the royal bodyguard corps and served as a powerful military force as well as political advisors. It's important to recognize that the name *Amazon* was given to them by European colonizers as an homage to the legendary Amazons of classical mythology. They called themselves *Mino,* which meant *our mothers* in the Dahomey language; this might just make them the perfect ancestor archetype.

Think of some other famous warriors who have lived in the past. Women like Boadicea of the Iceni and Grace O'Malley, the pirate queen, or men such as Alexander the Great or Leonidas of Sparta are all powerful archetypes you can call upon. Just remember that like other non-archetypal ancestors, these historical figures were once living, which means they had their flaws, as the rest of us do. Do your research, and make sure you're not calling upon an archetype that would be a Problem Ancestor if you bumped into them in your family tree. If they *are* problematic for whatever reason, figure out how you'll bypass those shortcomings and imperfections.

The Mother or Queen

You'll encounter the archetype of the mother or queen in every cultural system. The mother isn't just someone who gives birth; she also nurtures and protects. She shows us the kinder, gentler side of humanity but don't mistake that for weakness. The mother brings us abundance and bounty, as well as the security and stability of the home. In her aspect as queen, she takes responsibility for the well-being and welfare of those around her, whether they are blood relatives or not, and offers care and guidance with her decision-making skills.

The mother archetype can be useful to work with in cases where you need to feel a little bit nurtured and loved unconditionally, or if you feel as though you need to offer a bit of extra protection to those under your care. However, she does have some pretty high expectations, much like real-life mothers do. She can place a little more pressure on us than we really want to deal with and may even project her disappointment in us when we fail to meet her standards, which can be hard to live up to. However, the mother is a wonderful supporter of new endeavors, so if you're looking to birth something new into your world—a business, a creative project, or a side hustle—the mother will totally have your back.

Mothers abound in mythology and folklore; of course, some have their down sides, so be selective about the ones you call upon. Perhaps the most famous mother/queen of all is Mary, the mother of Jesus. Setting aside the religious aspect of her story for just a moment, it's clear that she's the very embodiment of the divine feminine. Although her status as sacred virgin is widely disputed, many people—women in particular—believe she symbolizes healing, love, and power, in addition to the very light within the human soul and our collective longing for redemption.

Most cultures have a goddess associated with motherhood and abundance, fertility and fruitfulness. Look into the legends of your family's cultures. Can you work with Demeter or Ceres, from the classical Greek and Roman legends? If your ancestry is based in the Celtic-language lands, consider calling upon Brigid, the Irish goddess who protects women in childbirth and serves as the guardian of the domestic hearth fires.

For badass historical moms, you've got centuries upon centuries of amazing and powerful women to choose from. My 24th great grandmother was a wife and mother of kings, but she was also a shrewd tactician who rode in the Crusades and one of the wealthiest women of the Middle Ages. During her lifetime, she ruled England on behalf of her sons, Richard the Lionheart and his younger brother, John Lackland, my direct ancestor. Is it any wonder I've got Eleanor of Aquitaine on my altar?

Are you of Native American ancestry? Explore the journeys of Sacagawea, a mother who carried her newborn infant strapped to her back as she guided Lewis and Clark on their famous trek. Not much is known about Sacagawea, but she was part of a branch of the Shoshone Nation; at various points in her expedition, she protected her baby from a capsizing boat, swarms of mosquitoes, and a host of other illnesses that plagued the crew members on the trip across North America.

Sojourner Truth once said, *I am the seed of the free, and I know it. I intend to bear great fruit.* Born and raised in slavery, her owners married her off and she began having children; by the time she was thirty she'd given birth to five. One day, she took her infant daughter and walked away to freedom, leaving behind the farm in Ulster County, New York, where she was enslaved. When she learned that her five-year-old son had been sold to a plantation in Alabama, she went to court to have him freed; Sojourner Truth was one of the first women of color to sue a white man in court and win. She became a powerful voice for the abolition movement in the nineteenth century.

The Father or King

Like the mother/queen archetype, the father or king appears in every cultural mythos. The father or king symbolizes power, energy, strength, and the ability to take control over our lives and the things that happen to us. He doesn't think the world revolves around him, but his confidence, sense of purpose, and emotional well-being give him a sense of harmony that others come to rely on for security and stability. Don't be misled, however—while the father is manly and masculine, he's also sensitive and thoughtful. A true father and king is the opposite of toxic masculinity—he's open to emotion, feelings, and communication. In Jungian thought, the father/king is linked closely to the warrior and the sage archetypes.

You might want to call in the ancestral archetype of the father if you need help in making decisions, or if you feel a need to take back control of your life. The king or father knows exactly who he is and what he stands for; he's got a code and principles, so when a crisis pops up, he's the guy you want at your back. He tempers his decisions with his own experience; his practical wisdom is born from making his own mistakes. The father or king will guide you toward doing what is fair and just; he'll show you how to do the right thing for the right reason when the time is right.

Who are some mythological and folkloric badass dads or kings you can work with? What about King Arthur, who led his knights of the round table? No one knows for sure if there was a real Arthur, although it's possible he was a Rome-affiliated military leader; he's credited with protecting Britain from a Saxon invasion around the fifth century. During the ninth century, a Welsh monk named Nennius wrote *Historia Brittonum* that detailed many battles in which Arthur allegedly fought, positioning the king of Camelot as a valiant and noble man. Later works by Geoffrey of

Monmouth, who added the Merlin part of the legend, helped to create King Arthur's archetypal origin story.

Throughout history, the father/king has been exemplified in the role of lawmaker—after all, they're the ones who provide order and structure. One of the most famous of these men was Hammurabi, the ancient Babylonian king. He created a code that became the first written set of laws in history, possibly the earliest that operated on the presumption of innocence rather than guilt. These laws, appropriately called the *Code of Hammurabi,* covered all areas of personal and public life—from trade and commerce and bread baking to religious practice and military service—for the people of Mesopotamia.

There are also protective dads out there, although it's important to avoid those who are so overprotective that they end up being horrible. The Emperor Charlemagne fathered at least twenty children, legitimate and not so much. However, he made sure all of his children were acknowledged and properly educated—including the girls, which was unheard of in Charlemagne's time, the eighth century.

Other father/king archetypes from history include men like Franklin Delano Roosevelt, whose inspiring words after the attack on Pearl Harbor inspired a nation, reassuring millions they would be safe, and helped shaped America with a sense of purpose and strength. Nelson Mandela spoke of power and freedom despite spending nearly three decades as a political prisoner. He served as a father figure for many in his native South Africa. Born into slavery, Frederick Douglass escaped and became an active abolitionist. Douglass had five children of his own, and famously said: *It is easier to build strong children than to repair broken men.*

The Trickster

The trickster archetype appears just about everywhere; nearly every culture has a trickster legend. While these figures can obviously spread chaos, tricksters can come in handy in spiritual workings. Tricksters are often deliberate rule-breakers, but ultimately the change they bring about is (usually) positive. In many mythologies, tricksters become cultural heroes. It's important to acknowledge that not all tricksters are the same, nor do they have the same motivations; archetypes carry traits valued within their own unique cultural contexts.

So why on earth would you bother working with an archetype that causes chaos and mischief? Sometimes, that's the only type of energy that can help you. If you need advice about how to deal with a tricky situation, where you've got the best of intentions but might have to do something sketchy to reach the outcome, the trickster is the perfect archetype to call in for ancestral workings. They're highly valuable for bringing us illumination and a sense of balance, by way of destruction and creation.

In Greek mythology, the titan Prometheus decided to steal fire from the gods and gift it to human beings. He already had a reputation as a clever trickster and, in addition to handing over fire, he also gave people the skill of metalworking. Zeus, the king of the Olympian gods, was not happy about any of this, so he ordered Prometheus to be chained to a rock where an eagle flew up every day to eat his liver.

West African stories tell the tales of Anansi, who is crafty and shrewd but ultimately benign—like many folk figures in African stories, Anansi uses clever language to deconstruct the restrictions that society puts on him. Associated with the spider, Anansi is connected to skill and wisdom in his speech and often appears as subversive; however, he always manages to put one over on those who might try to keep him down.

The character of Robin Hood of European folklore can be considered a trickster. He takes from the rich to give to the poor and causes disruption of the social hierarchy in the name of justice and fairness. When the heist has ended, what's left is simple honesty, and a trajectory toward change in society.

To find a trickster archetype in history, look at people who have disrupted convention for the greater good. Leonardo da Vinci did things that seemed really weird to his contemporaries, broke most of the rules of the art and science worlds, rarely finished his work, and had an eye for destruction. And yet his legacy lives on, and the work he began so many centuries ago laid the groundwork for developments in science, art, and mathematics.

Legendary blues guitarist Robert Johnson could well be the quintessential trickster archetype in history. Not much is known about Johnson's early years, and he died at only twenty-seven years old. However, tall tales abound, perhaps the best known that he made a deal with the devil at a crossroads in order to achieve musical greatness. Despite his early death, Johnson was a progenitor of the Delta blues sound, and his work influenced artists to come for decades—bands like the Rolling Stones, Led Zeppelin, and Fleetwood Mac have all given him credit for his impact on their musical styles. Some folklorists see the story of Johnson's supernatural encounter as not involving the Christian devil or Satan but the West African figure Legba who is well known as a trickster and associated with crossroads.

The Explorer

The archetype of the explorer can be found in many forms, but the common thread is that explorers have a need for purpose and meaning. They're often individualistic and feel a need to be free from established constraints. Refusing to be caged in, the explorer archetype is one that speaks to our need for freedom, unconventionality, and adventure.

Consider working with the explorer archetype as an ancestral guide if you need help with issues related to starting new projects, whether they're professional or personal in nature. Because of the explorer's association with self-discovery, work with this archetype can be valuable when you're just trying to figure out your own sense of purpose, and determining who you really are, who you want to be, and where you want to go. The explorer is a pioneer who blazes new trails where no one has set foot before.

In folklore is a cornucopia of explorer archetypes to work with from around the world. Ancient epics have thousands of stories about wandering adventurers—think of Jason and the Argonauts, or any other classic tale about someone who is sent off on a series of seemingly random quests just to fulfill their own destiny.

Much of the modern world has developed because of explorers. Although exploration and colonization frequently go hand in hand, the fact remains that there are plenty of explorer and adventurers out there who changed the way we saw the rest of the world. The English sea captain, Sir Francis Drake, circumnavigated the globe in the sixteenth century and battled against the Spanish Armada. He was so successful that the Spanish branded him as a pirate, and King Philip II offered a reward to anyone who could capture or kill Drake.

Black Cat, the chief of a Mandan village, was a Native American explorer who lived around the same time as Lewis, Clark, and

Sacagawea were charting their way across the continent. Black Cat was curious about the everyday fabric of the life of the white settlers who had come to his land. He met with Lewis and Clark and shared anecdotes and trading stories so that he could learn about this strange new culture.

Alexander Hamilton fits the explorer archetype well. Raised in the Caribbean by a widowed mother who left him an orphan at a young age, Hamilton wanted to be something more than he was and to see the rest of the world. His insatiable quest for knowledge led him to King's College in New York State, where he soon became involved with the Loyalist movement, and hobnobbed with the men who would become America's founding fathers. The rest, as they say, is history.

Today's explorers may not be circumnavigating the globe in frigates, but they're constantly making new discoveries in a variety of ways. They're the scientists—the Marie Curies and Jonas Salks of the world—who are innovators in their fields. They're entrepreneurs like Steve Wozniak and Steve Jobs, two guys who built a computer in a garage and turned their idea into one of the modern world's tech giants. They are astronauts and undersea explorers like Neil Armstrong, the first man to set foot on the moon and oceanographer Robert Ballard, the first to see *Titanic* since 1912. The free thinkers of the psychedelic exploration movement—Timothy Leary, Ram Dass, and the creative minds from the beat generation all sought to discover new spiritual frontiers in their own ways.

The Rebel

We find the rebel archetype in all kinds of mythologies and legends, and each of us has self-identified with the rebel at some point in our lives. The rebel serves a valuable purpose in the world of archetypes, because much like the explorer, they are free from the typical constraints of society. It's not that a rebel is unaware of those constraints; they simply don't allow themselves to be held by them. The rebel brings about freedom by way of dissent and justice by way of rebellion.

Work with a rebel archetype when you're facing conflict from the forces around you, dealing with oppressive leaders or rulers, or standing up for something you believe in—especially if it's not considered a popular ideal. The rebel can help us bring about innovation and change, reform and renewal, and ultimately, transformation. Folkloric rebels appear in just about every culture. From characters like Reynard the Fox to Zorro to Batman, the rebel goes against the grain, breaks the rules as needed, and fights for the rights of those who can't fight on their own.

For historical examples of the rebel, just think about the people who founded or changed most countries—they say dissent is the foundation of history, and that's where people like Paul Revere come in. He was a silversmith and artisan, as well as an early industrialist. His work with the Sons of Liberty as well as his famous midnight ride helped shape the course of American history.

The rebel is a free spirit, and often a creative one who lives under a set of unconventional guidelines they set for themselves. Artist Frida Kahlo was a revolutionary in the worlds of both art and politics. The raw and bloody political content of some of her paintings was completely beyond the realm of normal for female artists of her time, and she brought to the spotlight a portrait of Mexican women's woes, pain, and self-determination. Although pop culture has commodified and commercialized Frida's life and art, in life she was a rebel and outspoken anarchist.

Anne Lister, better known as Gentleman Jack, was a nineteenth-century Yorkshire landowner who broke all kinds of rules, striding around town in a top hat and operating coal mines instead of sitting around politely doing embroidery in a drawing room. Intellectually adventurous, Anne delved into the world of reform politics, kept up with Darwin's newest discoveries, and collected minerals from her travels around the globe. Perhaps even more subversively, Anne kept numerous diaries—totaling more than five million words—written in code and detailing her romantic and sexual escapades with society women. Although *Jack* was derogatory Yorkshire slang for a lesbian, Anne didn't care—she embraced the nickname, merrily seduced ladies she found appealing, and eventually had a secret marriage ceremony with heiress Ann Walker, who lived with her as a wife for years.

The Lover

Another archetype we may look to for ancestral guidance is that of the lover. The lover isn't so much about romance and sexuality (although they can obviously be called upon for either) as they are about giving, commitment, and faithfulness. The lover connects to the deeper emotions we feel and experiences empathy for others. This is a person who thrives on receiving and expressing love in whatever form it may take.

If you need advice or guidance related to emotional connections, personal empowerment, or the way in which others view you, the lover archetype is one to think about working with. The lover puts themselves in other people's shoes to help give perspective, not only about ourselves but also with those we care about and who care about us in return. This is an archetype that is passionate about and committed to feelings and sensitivity, as well as understanding the strength found in both intimacy and vulnerability. The lover can often appear as a cautionary tale—think of

Romeo and Juliet. Sure, they were lovers … but they also died tragically because they couldn't communicate effectively. The lover archetype encourages us to speak about what we need on an emotional level.

Look at goddesses like Aphrodite/Venus, Mami Wata, or Inanna for mythological examples of the lover archetype. The Greek Aphrodite—or Venus to the people of ancient Rome—was associated with love and beauty. Although she often meddled in the affairs of mortals, she was also a big advocate of the pursuit of pleasure. It sometimes got her in trouble—like that one time she had an affair with Ares, who had to pay her husband a fine for the privilege—but Aphrodite's commitment to love in its many forms was empowering for her.

The West African figure Mami Wata appears in the legends of Nigeria and Senegal and is a water spirit associated with both fidelity and sexual relationships. She has a tendency to take over the hearts and souls of those who she finds appealing—male and female—and she brings them home to her magical realm. Once released, her lovers often find a renewed sense of emotional clarity.

Historical lovers abound—think of all the incredible things people have done in the name of love, emotion, and matters of the heart! The most evolved lovers are those who are willing to let things go for the benefit of those they care about. The British King Edward VIII caused a major constitutional crisis when he abdicated the throne just so he could marry divorced American socialite Wallis Simpson.

Cleopatra, Queen of Ptolemaic Egypt, was known as quite the seductress; she had relationships with and bore children by both Julius Caesar and Mark Antony. After Caesar's death, she refused to capitulate to the new emperor, Octavian. Her love for famous men often overshadows her contributions to the political landscape, education, and intellect of the times, but it was her refusal to abandon Antony that ultimately led to her death. A woman of principle and passion, Cleopatra changed history in the name of love both for Antony and the people of Egypt.

Nine
DIVINATION WITH YOUR BADASS KIN

One of the most powerful and valuable ways to work with our ancestral connections is to ask them for guidance. Their wisdom can prove insightful, and they can help us make decisions and understand things that have previously been beyond our reach. But how do we ask them these questions? Do you just shout out *Hey, Uncle Egbert, should I quit my job or stay put?* You certainly can. And there's a chance you'll get an answer, if Uncle Egbert is feeling particularly chatty.

A more productive method is to engage in some good old-fashioned divination wherein you speak to the people you consider kin and clan. In addition to providing you with ideas and insight, calling your ancestors for divination helps to form the relationship you want to develop with your ancestors. After all, you're having a conversation, and that's how you facilitate a connection.

There are many different types of divination you can use in your ancestral practice, but you may find that you're more gifted in one method than others. Figure out which works best for you and your abilities—and remember, just like with any other skill set, practice makes perfect!

When you're doing divination—whichever method you choose—it's a good idea to keep a journal. Write down everything you see, hear, and experience. This is valuable for a couple of reasons. First of all, as human beings, we tend to forget stuff. Writing it down will allow you to revisit it later, and help you remember what you saw. Also, there may be messages that seem to have nothing at all to do with anything you're asking about, but that's okay—it is common to get messages in divination that answer a question we didn't ask but perhaps should have. Maybe you'll suddenly think about someone you haven't seen in decades or hear a snippet of a song that once had meaning to you. Jotting these things down will allow you to figure out patterns in your messages; even if something doesn't make sense at the time, it might in the future.

Scrying

Scrying is the art of staring into something—often a shiny surface, but not always—for the purpose of divination. As you scry, you'll begin to get visions that you can interpret intuitively. There are a number of different ways to do this, but all of them should be performed at your ancestor altar—after all, that's where your badass people are hanging out in your home.

You've probably watched movies that included an old fortune teller peering into a crystal ball while she hisses, "Cross my palms with silver!" in some sort of vaguely Eastern European accent. The reality is that people all over the world have used crystals and glass for scrying for thousands of years. By focusing on the ball, which is usually made of a clouded glass, you may be able to see visions that foretell not only the future but unknown aspects of the present and past, which makes it a perfect delivery method for scrying with your ancestors.

Another popular method of scrying, sometimes called hydro-mancy, involves the use of a bowl of water. Nostradamus put himself into a trance to interpret the visions he saw in a bowl of water, and we know how well that turned out—he had plenty of predictions to share. You might even want to try incorporating the reflections of the moon into your scrying—if you're someone who feels more aware and alert during the moon's fullest phase, this might be a good method to try! In some forms of water scrying, the practitioner has a bowl of water in front of them and then touches the flat surface of the water with a wand or a finger. This creates a ripple effect, which can change the types of images that are seen.

With fire scrying—which is exactly what it sounds like—you can stare into the flames of a fire to see what sort of visions might appear. As with other methods of scrying, this is very intuitive. By relaxing your mind and focusing only on the flames, you may get messages telling you what you need to know. Watch as the fire flickers and flashes and look for images in the flames. Some people see clear and specific images, while others see shapes in the shadows, mere hints of what is within. Look for images that seem familiar or for those that may repeat in a pattern. You may even hear sounds as you watch the fire that are not just the crackling of wood, the roar of larger flames, or the snapping of embers. Some people report hearing faint voices singing or speaking in the fire. Do you hear your ancestors calling you?

Finally, you can try using a scrying mirror. This is not a true mirror, but a piece of glass that has been painted matte black on the back side to create a shiny and reflective surface on the front. You can make one with any piece of glass—raid your local thrift store to pick up a picture frame. Remove the glass from the frame, clean it thoroughly, and lay it on a piece of cardboard or newspaper outside with the back side up. Use matte black spray paint—don't use glossy paint, you won't like the results—and gently spray the glass, moving evenly across from side to side. You'll probably need to use three to four coats to completely cover the glass. Check by holding the glass up to a light: if you don't see any light shining through the black, you've got enough paint.

Once the paint is dry, put the glass back in the frame. If you want, you can embellish the frame around the outer edges. Add symbols of your own magical belief system, names of ancestors you'd like to work with, or a poem or phrase that resonates with you. Once you've got it back in the frame, place it on your altar, and get ready to scry.

Whichever method you've decided to use, you can do this simple scrying ritual to help move forward with ancestor communication.

Sit at your ancestor altar and make yourself comfortable. Light your candles, close your eyes, and take some time to immerse yourself in the connection to your family. While some people like to have music playing quietly in the background, others find it to be distracting. If you think music might influence any information and/or visions you receive, skip it.

You can begin by calling out to your ancestors, like so:

I call to you, my family, my people, my blood. I call to my mothers and fathers, my grandmothers and grandfathers, my aunts and uncles and cousins, going back generation upon generation, to the beginning of time. I call you to me, and ask that you may walk with me, watch over me, and offer me guidance with this question that troubles me.

If there's a specific individual you want to reach out to, you can address them by name to get their attention. It's also a good idea to tell them *why* you've chosen them. Are they someone who was brave or strong or wise? *I call to you, Great-great-grandfather Jeremiah, and ask for your guidance and insight and wisdom. I call to you, that you might bring your courage and resolve to help me as I work to face this challenge.*

When you are ready to begin scrying, open your eyes. Position yourself so that you can look into whatever you're going to be scrying with—a bowl of water, a candle flame, your mirror, etc. Stare into the reflective surface, resting your gaze at a point just before the glass, looking for patterns, symbols or pictures—and don't worry if you blink; this isn't a staring contest. Worrying about blinking will be distracting, so it's fine to do so. As you look into the surface, think about the question at hand, and focus on it.

Should I go back to school, even though I'm in my forties?

Am I right to be distrustful of this new person in my life, even though there's no logical reason to feel this way?

I need guidance because I am lost and don't know what to do with myself next.

At some point, you'll start to see images moving, or perhaps even words forming. You may have random thoughts pop spontaneously into your head. Spend as much time as you like gazing into your scrying surface—it may be just a few minutes or even an hour. Stop when you begin to feel restless, if you're distracted by mundane things, or if you get the sense that your ancestors have stopped responding. Sometimes they run out of things to say, or they've given you all the advice they're prepared to deliver at this time.

Pendulum Divination

A pendulum is one of the simplest and easiest forms of divination, and it's quick and stress-free to use, which means it should probably be an important part of your badass ancestral tool kit. Pendulum divination works best for questions with two potential outcomes—

yes/no, stay/go, thing one/thing two, etc.—although if used with a spirit board, you can sometimes parse out more comprehensive answers.

You can purchase pendulums commercially, either online or in your favorite local metaphysical shop, but making one of your own is super easy. Typically, most people use a crystal, but you can use any object you like. Do you still have your great-grandmother's platinum wedding ring from 1920? What about that odd stone with the hole in it that you found in a box of family postcards from Ireland? To turn an object into a pendulum, use something with some weight—a ring or other piece of jewelry is perfect for this—and a light chain or a length of string, ideally between ten and fourteen inches long. Attach one end of the chain to the ring so that it's secure and will hang freely.

To charge your pendulum overnight, place it in the moonlight or in a bowl on your altar. In some magical belief systems, consecrated water or sea salt are used, but don't immerse your pendulum in anything that might cause corrosion or damage.

Next, you'll want to calibrate your charged pendulum to see how it works. Hold it by the free end of the chain so that the ring or other weighted object is dangling from your hand. Keep it perfectly still; you might want to rest your elbow on a table or your altar. Next, ask your pendulum a simple yes or no question to which you already know the answer is yes, such as: *Do I live in Oklahoma? Is my dog named Brutus? Am I an only child?* Keep an eye on the pendulum. When it starts to move, pay attention to how it swings: forward to backward, side to side, or some other direction. This will indicate your pendulum's yes direction.

Repeat the process, but this time, ask a question with a definite no answer. It's a good idea to try each of these a couple of different times with various questions, just to see how your pendulum is going to respond. Some swing enthusiastically, others in tiny increments, and still others seem to dance around in circular patterns. And some pendulums might not do much of anything unless the answer is something you *really* need to know. Regardless, once you've got your pendulum charged and calibrated, you can start using it for divination.

You can certainly ask simple yes/no questions of your ancestors using your pendulum while at your altar, but you can also do so much more. Try using your pendulum in tandem with a spirit or divination board that has the alphabet imprinted on it. Ask your ancestors for insight and answers and see toward which letters and numbers the pendulum swings.

Have you lost something important? Ask your kinfolk to help you locate it and follow your pendulum like a dowsing rod until you've tracked down the item. You can also sketch out a map of the area in which you think the item might be hiding and hold the pendulum over it so that your ancestors can direct you to the right spot, if they're so inclined.

Ancestor Oracle Cards

Most people have heard of tarot cards, but oracle cards are growing in popularity. Tarot cards are fairly universal; they've got seventy-eight cards that fall into the categories of either the major or minor arcana. Major arcana cards explore our spiritual experiences, and the four suits of the minor arcana help offer insight into our life stories. Although the artwork varies from one deck to the next, the messages are often the same.

Oracle cards, however, are much freer in form; a deck can have as many cards as the creator wants and any meaning that the creator assigns to them. They're much easier to learn than tarot's structured symbolism and can often offer guidance and perspective when you need it the most. Each card has an image as well as words that associate the image with a particular concept or idea. Here is where your badass ancestors are about to come in very handy.

Anyone can make an oracle deck, but it's often hard to find images that are both related to one another and have meaning to the creator. So why not use images of your ancestors?

First, start thinking about the people in the photos you have access to. Look at the pictures of your ancestors—after all, they're sitting right there on your altar! What comes to mind when you look at each of them? Think of a few words or phrases to represent each of them; don't hesitate to ask them for guidance in this. Here are some examples of people you might find in your family tree and phrases that may come to mind:

- Intrepid and Adventurous: a photo of your great-great-great aunt, who traveled the world alone when women weren't supposed to do such things, perched on the hood of a Model T

- Charity and Generosity: The image you found of a long-dead school teacher in your family tree who founded a home for unwed mothers and orphaned children

- Focus and Hard Work: A picture of the building in which your great-something grandfather started a business that remains in the family to this day

- Bravery and Loyalty: That postcard mailed from Bastogne in 1944, featuring one of your ancestors and the men with whom he shared a foxhole

Once you've figured out which images you want to use and how many cards you want to include in your oracle deck, the possibilities are limitless. Scan your photos so you have digital images and print them on heavy duty card stock. Letter each of them with the phrases and words you associate with each picture. If it helps you keep people's identities straight, add labels with names—you can also include an abbreviation in the corner explaining how they're related to you. Use simple codes like *2gm* for a great-great-grandmother, or *1C2xR* to represent your first cousin, two times removed. You may want to laminate the cards when you're done, for more durability.

Remember that creating something as personal as an ancestor oracle deck is a magical act. As you write on each card, take the time to hold it, speak to the ancestor, and let them know you're ready and willing to hear the wisdom they can share with you. Once you've finished your deck of oracle cards—and remember, this can be an ongoing process as you connect with more ancestors in your tree—keep them in a place of honor on your altar. Mine live wrapped in a bit of silk, tucked happily into a small wooden box that I decoupaged with an image of the castle where one of my nineteenth-century ancestors worked as a servant.

To use your oracle cards, hold them in your hands and ask questions. Ask for insight, calling out to your people. Shuffle the cards, rearranging them until they feel right, and then remove a card to see who has a message for you. Focus on that individual and what they represent to you, and let their messages guide you.

Divination with Runes or Staves

Divination methods vary around the world, but no matter where your people are from, odds are good they had some sort of badass way of doing it. For people of Norse, Germanic, or Scandinavian backgrounds, runes are a popular method. Although you don't have to be of Norse ancestry to use them, it will help you to study up on Norse culture, mythology, and spirituality to have a more complete and rounded understanding of what the runes actually mean. Although their meanings and how they relate to the situation at hand can sometimes be a bit puzzling, most people who work with runes find the best way to use them is to ask a specific question based on the current situation. When working with your ancestors, you can ask them to guide your rune work.

There are several variations on the Norse runes, but typically they consist of stones, bone, or pieces of wood, each engraved with one of the two dozen symbols from the Elder Futhark, the old Germanic runic alphabet. It gets its name from the first six letters, which spell out the word *futhark*. Other versions include the Anglo-Saxon *futhorc*, which contains thirty-three symbols, Turkish and Hungarian runes, and even a style based on the ancient Etruscan alphabet.

Each symbol has a deeper spiritual meaning, as well as a practical one. For instance, the first in the series is the rune *fehu*, which looks a bit like the letter F. It symbolizes wealth and cattle, but also the god Freyr, who is associated with prosperity, divine kingship, and peace. The symbol *tiwaz* is representative of the god Tyr, who made a great sacrifice, but it also can mean honor, justice, and authority.

Like other forms of divination, reading the runes is not "telling the future"; it is a tool for guidance in which you ask your ancestors to provide you with their insight and wisdom. Some people believe that the selections made by drawing runes are answers that confirm what we already know in our hearts. Regardless of whether or not you see it as new information or simply validation, try asking your ancestors for advice when you draw rune stones.

In the Celtic-language lands, staves were often used that featured straight-lined symbols known as the Ogham alphabet. Although we don't know today how our Celtic ancestors might have used staves, or sticks (there are very few written records), there are a number of ways that they can be read and interpreted.

The Ogham alphabet originally contained twenty symbols, and five more were added later on. Each Ogham symbol corresponds to a letter or sound, in addition to a tree or wood; like the Norse runes, each has come to be associated with various spiritual meanings and elements of the human experience. For instance, *luis* (pronounced *loosh*), a straight vertical line that has two horizontal arms off to the right, is connected to the letter L and the rowan tree. It also represents insight and blessings, as well as protection against enchantment and evil spirits. In parts of Ireland and the Celtic world, stones carved with Ogham symbols still stand today.

To use runes or staves, request help and illumination from your ancestors regarding a particular issue, and then look at the influences of the past and present. In addition, look at what will happen if you follow your current trajectory. The future is changeable based on your own choices, so by allowing your ancestors to point out cause and effect, you can look at potential outcomes.

If you'd like your people to help you with this divination method, the simplest way to draw a rune or stave (or several) is to place them in a bag so that you can't see them. Close your eyes and ask your ancestors to join you. Petition them for their wisdom: *Hail, my kin and clan, my people, my bloodline. Open my eyes so I can see my path. Show me the past, and the present so I can make the right choices in the future. Illuminate and educate me, enlighten and guide me.*

With your eyes closed, draw three runes or staves, one at a time, and place them on your altar in a row. Open your eyes, and see which symbols are in front of you. The first one will represent both past influences, and an overall analysis of the root of your issue. The one in the center symbolizes the challenges you are facing. The final stone is the action your ancestors want you to take to solve your dilemma.

As is typical with divination, sometimes the messages are cryptic and will take a bit of self-evaluation—and probably some self-criticism—before they make sense. Don't be afraid to delve deep to figure out the more obscure symbolism you're seeing—the important part is, how does it relate to the situation at hand? You may not even see the answers you want right away—which is why it's a good idea to write down which runes or staves you've pulled, so you can go back and revisit them later for further study.

When finished, thank your ancestors for sharing their insight with you. Leave them an offering in tribute: *Hail, my kin and clan, my people, my bloodline. Thank you for your wisdom; I have plenty to think about, and value the advice you have given. I am grateful for the chance to learn from you and leave you this wine as thanks.*

Casting Bones and Stones

In places ranging from Asia to Africa to Appalachia, casting bones and stones has been the traditional method of divination. In this technique, small items such as bones, stones, shells, coins, and other trinkets are thrown, typically onto a cloth, and the pattern in which they fall gives the answer to the question at hand. Casting bones is a uniquely personal system of divination—there's no One True Way to do it—so if this is something that really speaks to you,

I'd recommend asking your ancestors for guidance as to what sorts of things they'd like to see you include.

To make your own casting set, start with a black cloth or mat about two feet square—it can even be smaller if you'd like, but I've found that 18 inches across is the ideal minimum. Some traditions use an animal hide or a wooden board for this; the choice is yours. You might want to mark your cloth with two circles, one inside another; in many bone throwing systems, the items that land inside the smaller circle are the things that matter most, those that fall into the larger circle are indirectly involved, and anything outside the circle doesn't count at all. You can also do this with a single circle, or even an overlapping pair in a Venn diagram. Again, casting bones is very personal, and no two systems are alike.

Next, you'll need a bag or basket to keep your bones and other curios in. The meanings you attach to each bone, shell, or stone is completely up to you, but it's important to be consistent. Gather a collection—and this will take some time—of small bones, trinkets, beads, coins, and more. There's no limit as to how many items you can use, but it may be a good idea to start small, with thirteen or less. The point is to collect items naturally, as you go about your day to day life, walking in the woods, exploring the alley behind your office, or even as you mow the yard. You can always add to them as you become more adept at asking your ancestors for guidance with bone readings. Here are some things you might want to add into your bone throwing kit:

- *Seashells:* cowrie shells represent divination in many African diasporic traditions, but you can use others if they speak to you.

- *Shiny coins:* silver works best for some people, others like pennies.

- *Small bones:* deer knuckles, skulls from small animals, and even birds' wishbones.

- *Stones:* use stones that feel magical or are associated with a place your ancestors might have lived, or crystals with special correspondences, like quartz or hematite.

- *A small key:* these often represent new opportunities.

- *Beads:* do you have some large beads from an ancestor's jewelry? What about a bead with protective symbols on it, like the Hamsa hand or the evil eye?

- Other curios like a pair of bone dice, a poker chip or gaming token, political buttons, dehydrated roots or animal claws, an empty shell casing, a sliver of tile or brick, nails or safety pins, bits of hardware, large seed pods, or even small pinecones.

After collecting all the pieces you want to gather, sit at your ancestor altar and hold each piece, one at a time, in your hands. Close your eyes and ask your kinfolk to tell you what that individual piece means. Does that coin mean prosperity, or does it mean luck? That empty shell casing might mean violence, or it might mean a successful hunt. The meanings are as varied as the items you collect, so as your ancestors give you answers, write them down. Once you've gone through all of your items, you've got a full set for bone throwing divination.

To use them, scatter them on the mat you've prepared—as you do so, focus on your question at hand, and ask your ancestors to guide you. Look at the bones and other goodies, see where they have landed, and figure out what your people are trying to tell you.

Keep in mind that meanings can change over time, so allow yourself the luxury of some flexibility. Be sure to thank your ancestors each time you throw the bones and show your gratitude for the insight they've given.

Other Divination Methods

You don't have to restrict yourself to scrying, pendulums, stones, or oracle cards to ask your ancestors for advice. Is there another method you like to use? Explore the different divination methods that your ancestors might have used in the countries in which they lived. Is there something unique to an indigenous group that you're descended from, or a method of divination that is only found in that one small Hungarian village from which your great-grandmother's mother hailed?

In addition to asking questions of your ancestors during divination, you can utilize their wisdom for healing. Do you suffer from a chronic or unexplained illness? Are you feeling as though you lack mental or spiritual clarity, or that you're drifting without purpose? Perhaps you've got emotional issues that relate to trauma, or your relationships with your parents or children, or your sense of self-worth. Ask your ancestors to help you navigate the waters of recovery.

Ten
EATING WITH
YOUR ANCESTORS

Have you ever thought about eating like your ancestors did? There's been a recent shift toward cleaner eating, and many people find that by re-traditionalizing their diets, they feel better physically. In addition, there is spiritual benefit to eating the sorts of foods our ancestors would have. By eating the meals they might have made, we can connect to them across the centuries; after all, sharing a meal and breaking bread with someone was an act of hospitality and love, so what better way to make your people feel welcome than preparing a dish they might have traditionally eaten?

Although many of our kinfolk got their food by hunting, fishing, and harvesting, we may not need to do that today—although certainly, if you've got a place to grow a garden, you should go for it. What we can do is recreate the ancestral dishes by following a few simple principles when it comes to our food. Think about food in the cultural context appropriate to your ancestors and the time period and place they lived. What foods would have been available to them?

Ideally, ancestral food should be locally sourced and seasonal. It should be food that you can process at home, making dishes from scratch with your bare hands, instead of taken out of a box or can and stuck in the microwave. Think in terms of ingredients that can be taken from the water, the land, or the sky. Ancestral foods are the sorts of things that people enjoyed for hundreds of years, before electricity and refrigeration, and certainly before colonization. These ingredients don't need a label—after all, there shouldn't be any preservatives in a potato or a pork chop—and they don't require a lot of excess packaging. Eating ancestrally allows us to treat food as sacred, in a way that honors the farm-to-table or field-to-table process. It permits us to understand the path that our food has taken to get to our plate, and when we prepare it in a way that respects our culture, we can thank the food itself, the person who planted and harvested it, the earth and land, and our bloodline.

When you sit down to eat an ancestral meal, one that honors the generations that came before you, it's extremely helpful to begin with a prayer. If your family has a traditional meal blessing that they use on special occasions, you can certainly speak that one; if not, you can simply offer a prayer that honors the food you're about to consume, while making your ancestors feel that they are welcome guests at your table.

Food anthropology shows us that not only *what* people ate around the world has varied over time, but also *how* they ate. If you lived in Medieval Europe, for instance, the majority of your neighbors would have consisted of peasants, not the wealthy. Peasants lived off the land and worked hard day in and day out to grow their own crops, raise their own livestock, or hunt and fish for wild meat. White bread, made from wheat flour, was considered a delicacy, because it was a crop that required a lot of manure to grow properly—often, only the local lord had enough resources to produce wheat. Instead, you and the people around you would bake your bread from rye and barley, which was much easier to grow. If the grain harvest was poor, you might have to grind up dried beans or peas into your bread just to stretch the supply a little further. You might make a pot of a filling, oat-based stew called *pottage*, which included legumes and root vegetables. You'd keep chickens for fresh eggs, as well as pigs and sheep for meat, even using their blood to make black pudding. You might get lucky enough to have the occasional fish or cheese, and you probably drank milk from your own cow and water from the nearby river; if you lived in a village, you probably had a neighbor who made ale.

If you lived in a nation or culture within Africa you would have farmed a variety of grains, depending on which area you lived in. Like barley, these grains could be baked into bread or turned into soups or porridges that were rich and filling. If you lived in Nigeria or Ghana, you might grow millet or yams; your cousins in Libya, Mauritania, or other parts of Northern Africa probably processed their millet into couscous, which formed the base of many meals. If you were enterprising and patient, you could turn your grain into beer. In Ethiopia and Eretria, near Africa's Horn, teff was a staple; once harvested it was fermented before use in baking flatbread and thickening stews.

You and your neighbors probably had goats, sheep, and chickens for meat and eggs, and you fished in the rivers and streams. Fertile soil along the riverbanks made for good crop production, so vegetables were available for just about every meal—including yams in some areas, and new strains of rice. You'd indulge your sweet tooth with bananas and other fruits, and the starch-heavy plantain might be a staple of many of your meals. Best of all, you could grow coffee beans, which you'd chew for extra energy or dry and grind up to make a beverage.

In the American colonies, things were a little different—the southern region was able to grow crops year-round, so if you lived in the Carolinas or Georgia, you'd have fresh vegetables any time you liked. Coastal areas had ready access to seafood, like cod and mackerel, tuna and trout, clams and lobsters and oysters. People in colonial America typically ate three meals a day, with breakfast being a simple affair—you might indulge yourself in some tea, a bit of warm bread, or some cornmeal mush. Your midday meal, which you would probably call dinner, was the largest meal of the day and consisted of soup or stew, a couple of different types of meats, and lots of vegetables. Once the evening rolled around and you were done with your day's work, you'd have supper, which was lighter fare like cheese and bread, as well as leftover cold meat from your earlier meal. Refrigeration hadn't been invented yet, and hunting could be a challenge in the winter, so you would have preserved your meat by salting, drying, or smoking it. You'd have pickled vegetables to store for later and made preserves and jams with your fruit crops. You likely hung up flavorful herbs to dry, like basil and sage and dill. Your beverage of choice might have been tea, but if you could afford it, chocolate drinks and chicory coffee were popular as well.

The sort of foods you prepare for your ancestors will be as uniquely personal as your altar is. A sample menu for an ancestral meal honoring my Scottish heritage might include the sort of self-sufficient foods my people ate two hundred years ago: root vegetables like potatoes and turnips, fresh meat and fish, cabbage and leeks and onions, and oats as a staple grain. When I work with my ancestors who lived in nineteenth-century America on the far edges of the western frontier, I might prepare venison or ham hocks, corn and collard greens, dairy products like cheese and fresh butter and eggs, beans and carrots and okra.

If your ancestors ate foods that don't appeal to you at all, try finding a middle ground. After all, eating ancestrally is about honoring *them*, not satisfying your own craving for a frozen pizza. The recipes in this section are easy to prepare and use foods that might have existed when your great-something grandparents lived. Give them a try, make adjustments to meet your own family's needs, and try serving up a meal for your kinfolk!

Traditional Broth Stew

Broth stew is a staple of cooking and menus all around the world, but particularly in the United Kingdom. Your people could make a basic broth from whatever vegetables happened to be in season; depending on where you lived, and the time of the year, these might include root veggies like carrots and turnips, but also cabbage, onions, and leeks. Meat is almost always added as well—lamb or mutton provides an especially rich flavor, but you can use beef if you prefer. In many places, barley, split peas, or lentils were added to make the stew even more filling. To make it really savory, add bones to the pot while it simmers. Be sure to peel and dice your vegetables into uniform sizes for more even cooking.

- 2 T butter or lard
- 1 onion, diced
- 3 cloves garlic, minced
- 2 pounds lamb shoulder or your favorite cut of beef
- ½ C barley
- ½ C dried beans, lentils, or split peas
- 2 t salt
- 8 C vegetable broth
- 2 large carrots, diced
- 1 each rutabaga, turnip, and parsnip, diced

- 2 bay leaves (discard before serving)

- 4 sprigs rosemary

- 1 T fresh thyme

- 1 C shredded cabbage

- 1 leek, chopped

Melt the butter in your soup pot, on low heat, and then add the onions and garlic. Cook for about five minutes until soft. Add the lamb, the barley, beans, salt, and broth to your pot, and bring it to a boil. Reduce heat to simmer for two to three hours, and then add the carrot, rutabaga, turnip, and parsnip. Add the herbs, and simmer for another hour. Pull the lamb out, shred or cube it, and then return it to the pot, along with the cabbage and leek. Give it another hour of simmering, and then serve it up as part of a meal for your ancestors.

Pepper Pot Stew

During the days of colonial America, pepper pot stew was a popular dish, especially around Philadelphia after George Washington ordered it served up to his frozen troops at Valley Forge. It was well known as a hearty, nourishing meal. It's likely that Washington first became familiar with pepper pot stew during one of his visits to Barbados, where his brother Lawrence served him a local dish called *Cohobblopot*. Although colonial Americans discovered pepper pot by way of the West Indies, it has roots in African cuisine, and was brought to North America and the Caribbean through the transatlantic slave trade.

Since that time, pepper pot has evolved so that there are a few famous variants. The Philadelphia version, according to legend, was made with tripe; meanwhile, the Carolina stew often contained seafood such as crabs or oysters. In Norfolk, this soup was made with a pork loin and the addition of beans; as was typical in historical food preparation, each area used regional ingredients that were available to cooks at the time. The recipe included here, containing beef, is inspired by the Caribbean version.

- 1 T cooking oil
- 1½ pounds stew beef
- 4 quarts water or vegetable stock
- 1 pound spinach, mustard, or collard greens, chopped
- 4 potatoes, peeled and diced
- 1 medium African yam or taro root, peeled and diced
- 2 plantains, peeled and diced
- 1 ham hock or ½ pound sliced salted pork
- 2 long red peppers, chopped—use the hottest pepper you can stand; Scotch Bonnet is traditional with this stew
- 1 T freshly ground allspice
- 1 t fresh thyme, chopped
- 1 bay leaf (discard before serving)
- Salt and pepper to taste
- Cooked rice

Heat the oil and fry the beef in a large soup pot, and then add the water. Add the greens, potatoes, yam, plantains, ham hock, and the red peppers. Stir in the allspice, thyme, and bay leaf. Bring it to a boil, and then reduce heat, allowing it to simmer for 2 to 3 hours. Remove the ham hock, and serve in a bowl over rice, seasoned with salt and pepper. In some areas, small dumplings, shredded crab meat, or even bits of lobster are added in the last half hour of cooking. What do you think your ancestors would prefer?

Roots a la Creme

In the eighteenth century, root vegetables were a popular ingredient in many dishes because not only did they grow just about everywhere, they were easy to store and save for the cold winter months. Your ancestors could eat root vegetable meals nearly any time of the year. By blending them with a crème and herb reduction, simple carrots and parsnips were turned into a delectable dish. Variants of this recipe have been found in cuisine all around the world, and it appears in a French cookbook dating as far back as 1745.

- 4 large carrots, washed, peeled, and sliced
- 4 parsnips, washed, peeled, and chopped
- 1 stick of unsalted butter (don't use margarine)
- 4 small scallions, peeled and chopped
- 1 small onion, diced
- 3 cloves garlic, mashed
- ½ t basil
- ½ t thyme
- 1 T corn starch
- 1 C vegetable stock
- ½ t salt
- ½ t ground black pepper
- 3 large egg yolks
- 1 C heavy cream

Boil the carrots and parsnips for half an hour, until they're soft enough to jab with a fork. Drain and add to a large sauté pan with the butter, scallions, onion, garlic, and herbs. Stir well and allow to cook on medium heat for fifteen minutes. Add the corn starch and stock to thicken your dish, and then add salt and pepper. Reduce heat to simmer. In a separate bowl, whisk the egg yolks and blend in the cream. Pour over the vegetable mix and stir it in until smooth; be sure to remove it from the heat before it scorches!

Baked Spaghetti Squash

Squash is a versatile vegetable, and the spaghetti squash variety serves as a perfect substitute for pasta; it also seems to taste much richer. Native to central America, it made its way to China via trade routes, where it became a popular food in the nineteenth century. Now, it's found nearly everywhere, but it didn't seem to gain traction in the United States until World War II, when it became a staple of the suburban victory garden.

- 1 spaghetti squash
- 1 stick unsalted butter
- 4 cloves garlic
- ¼ C freshly grated Parmesan cheese
- 1 T basil
- 1 t oregano
- Pinch of salt and pepper to taste

Preheat your oven to 350° F. Cut the squash in half lengthwise and scoop out the seeds. Cut the stick of butter in half lengthwise, and place one half in each half of the squash. Lay the two squash halves side by side in a baking dish. Top evenly with garlic, Parmesan cheese, basil, oregano, salt, and pepper. Bake for one hour, and then remove your squash from the oven to cool. Scoop out the spaghetti-like strands and enjoy it as a side dish or top it with your ancestors' favorite sauce as part of your main course.

Herbal Butter Blends

The history of butter goes back almost as far as that of domesticating livestock. Several thousand years ago, people figured out they could take milk from their animals and turn it into a tasty spread. It has been used in religious ceremonies, burned for lamp fuel, and even smeared on the skin to protect against chafing from the chilly wind. Some societies, like the Greeks, saw butter as a divine gift that protected against evil. It's also been used as medicine, as both a poultice to treat burns, and massaged into the hair to make it healthy. You can make your own butter easily and add a bit of herbal goodness to it for extra flavoring. Serve it up on freshly baked bread when you're making an offering to your kinfolk, wherever they might be from.

- 1 quart heavy cream
- A pinch of salt

Let the cream sit overnight so that it will reach room temperature *but*—safety tip: don't leave it out more than 24 hours or it will spoil. Pour it into a large glass jar, about two-thirds full, add the salt, and then tighten the lid. Shake the jar for 20 to 30 minutes. Check it periodically; if the contents are getting too thick to shake, open the jar and stir the cream with a fork. Eventually, it will start to form yellow clumps. These clumps are butter, which means you're almost done! Drain any excess liquid out in a strainer; the liquid can be used in recipes calling for buttermilk.

Blend your butter with a combination of herbs, like:

- Dill Butter: Blend in 1 C fresh chopped dill.
- Savory Mustard Butter: Combine 2 T dry mustard with 1 C freshly chopped chives or onions.
- French Herb Butter: Mix together 2 T each tarragon, oregano, sage, and basil.
- Lemon Garlic Butter: Combine 2 T grated lemon zest with 1 T finely chopped parsley, ½ t ground black pepper, and 2 cloves of garlic, minced.

Keep your butter in the fridge; use it within a week.

Chicken and Couscous

Couscous is a grain that's been popular in African, Middle Eastern, and Mediterranean cooking as far back as the seventh century. Made from different types of local grains—everything from semolina to millet to farina—it's become a staple food in many areas, and because it's so versatile, you can use it as a base in just about any dish. One of the most popular ways to serve couscous is by topping it with a savory, rich blend of chicken, vegetables, and herbs. Would your ancestors appreciate a meal that's reminiscent of this part of the world?

- 1 C couscous, prepared
- 2 T olive oil
- 1 medium onion, chopped

- 1 t ground black pepper
- ½ t ground red pepper
- 1 t ground turmeric
- ½ t cinnamon
- 1 t ground cloves
- 1 t paprika
- 1 bay leaf (discard before serving)
- 4 large chicken breasts, boneless and skinless
- 16 ounces chickpeas, drained and rinsed
- 2 large tomatoes, chopped
- 1 zucchini, chopped
- 1 large carrot, chopped
- 2 C chicken broth

Heat the olive oil in a large saucepan, over medium heat, and add the onion, cooking until it's translucent. Mix in the black and red pepper, turmeric, cinnamon, cloves, paprika, and bay leaf. Add the chicken and cook until evenly browned. Add the chickpeas, vegetables, and chicken broth, and simmer on low heat for 45 minutes, or until the veggies are tender and the sauce has thickened. Salt to taste and serve over a bed of warm couscous.

Seasonal Greens

Although salad is something we often think of as a food we only eat when we're watching our calories, fresh greens and raw nuts, seeds, and other produce have been part of the human diet for hundreds of generations. Members of the cabbage family—which includes many dark greens—have been consumed the world over, although many didn't reach North America until the seventeenth century. A staple in many cultures, greens are full of rich nutrients and are delicious, to boot!

- ¼ C olive oil
- 4 cloves garlic, minced
- ½ C red onion, diced
- ½ C red pepper, diced
- 2 pounds collard, mustard, or spinach greens, washed and dried
- ½ C pine nuts, lightly toasted
- ½ C lemon juice
- Kosher salt and ground black pepper to taste

Heat the oil over medium heat in a large skillet, and add the garlic, onions, and red pepper. Sauté until soft and beginning to brown, and then add the greens. Allow them to cook down until they're wilted, turning and tossing them so they're evenly coated with the oil, about ten minutes. Remove from heat, and stir in the pine nuts, lemon juice, kosher salt and black pepper. Serve as a side or main dish.

Baked Apples

Apples are believed to have been around for most of recorded history. With dozens of different varieties, apples grow all over the world, but they seem to have originated around the Caucasus mountain region and traveled around the globe as our ancestors began to migrate. By the early eighteenth century, hundreds of new varieties had developed, thanks to Americans' love of propagating

hybrid species in their orchards. This recipe is based in part on a traditional German Christmas dish that's been served in many forms
for centuries, the *Bratapfel*, an apple stuffed with nuts, honey, and
plums. It's a delicious dessert that you can make any time of year,
especially if you think your ancestors might be fans of sweet treats.

- 6 of your favorite kind of apples—Fuji or Granny Smith
  are best
- ½ C apple cider
- ½ C brown sugar
- ½ C chopped walnuts or pecans
- ¼ C golden raisins
- ¼ C honey
- 1 t cinnamon
- 1 T allspice
- 3 T unsalted butter, sliced into six equal parts
- 1 T pure vanilla extract
- 2 C heavy cream
- 1 egg yolk
- 1 T brown sugar
- 1 t corn starch

Preheat your oven to 375° F. Remove the core from the apples
and hollow them out, leaving the bottom half-inch or so of the
apple intact; start with an apple corer to remove most of the center
and then use a sharp paring knife to widen the hollow. Make the
hollow as wide as possible; 1 to 2 inches wide will work best. After
you've hollowed out your apples, place them in a baking dish with
the apple cider in the bottom.

For the filling, combine the brown sugar, chopped nuts, raisins, honey, cinnamon, and allspice together in a bowl. Mix well, and then spoon it evenly into the hollow of each apple. Top each one with a slice of butter. Bake for 30 to 45 minutes so the apples are tender but not mushy. Remove from the oven and baste them with the cider from the bottom of the baking dish. Allow to cool for ten minutes before serving.

Top with a simple vanilla sauce, by warming the vanilla and heavy cream on low heat in a saucepan. In another pan, heat the egg yolk, brown sugar, and corn starch, whisking until smooth. Pour the cream mixture into the egg blend and continue stirring on low heat for ten minutes or until it thickens. Drizzle the sauce over your warm, freshly baked apples.

Soul Cakes

In many parts of the world, special breads or cakes are made as a gift for the spirits of the dead. You can use these in a silent supper, or simply put them together as an offering on your ancestor altar. After all, well fed ancestors tend to be very responsive to petitions and prayers. These cakes take many different names and shapes—in Europe, they're simply called soul cakes. In some areas, they were made as an unpretentious shortbread, and in others they were baked as tarts filled with chopped fruit, dates, or nuts. Still other regions made them of rice flour. Some styles of African cooking feature grains like amaranth, barley, or millet—what breads can you bake from these? In Mexico, *pan de Muertos* is traditional, and in the Netherlands, *ontbijtkoek* is a popular cakelike bread stuffed with nutmeg, honey, and pepper. Historically, a soul cake was made with whatever staple grain a particular community had available.

The true history of the soul cake and the practice of giving them away has been lost to the centuries. Some people say that they go back as far as the Druids; cakes were baked around the Samhain bonfire season. In other tales, soul cakes are used as an offering to placate any grumpy ghosts that might be loitering nearby. One thing is certain, which is that by around the eighth century, soul cakes became popular with the Christian church. Cakes were blessed and consecrated, so they could be given to poor travelers who approached the local monastery for sustenance.

Here's a recipe for a simple shortbread-style soul cake.

- 1 stick butter, softened
- ¼ C granulated sugar
- 1¼ C flour

Preheat oven to 350° F. Cream together the butter and sugar. Use a flour sifter to add the flour to the bowl and mix until smooth. Shape the dough into a flat circle about half an inch thick. Place on an ungreased baking sheet or baking stone, and poke lines with the tines of a fork to make eight separate wedges. Bake for 25 minutes or until the shortbread is light brown.

For something a little fancier, you can make a fruit-filled tart style soul cake. Make your favorite pie crust recipe, roll it out, and cut it into small circles using the top rim of a drinking glass, lightly dusted in flour. Use the circles to line a tray of muffin cups. Blend together two tablespoons melted butter, two tablespoons local honey, and 1 cup of mixed dried fruit. Scoop the fruit mixture into your muffin-sized pie crusts, and then bake for 15 minutes at 375° F.

Whatever type of cake you decide to make, place it as an offering on your altar as a gift for your ancestors to show you how much you appreciate them.

Eleven
YOUR BADASS
LEGACY

Someday, you may well be someone else's ancestor—and hopefully your descendants will look at your photos and journals, or maybe your ancient Tumblr and Instagram, and think *Wow, what a total badass!* That's why it's important to leave a valuable spiritual and genealogical legacy behind. From writing things down in journals, putting together a family recipe collection, and labeling photographs for future generations, as well as pre-death planning, there's a lot of stuff you need to think about. In the future, when your descendants have to dig through your belongings, why not at least cut them some slack and make it a little easier?

The best time to start thinking about what sort of legacy you'll leave behind is long before you shuffle off this mortal coil. You've got a lot of things you can do, but keep in mind that generations to come might be poring over your stuff someday. What do you want to leave them?

Share the Knowledge

Before you're dead and gone, why not encourage your family members to become as interested in genealogy and ancestor work as you are? Tell the stories you've uncovered as you uncover them. Share with your children and grandchildren as you sit down to dinner, or when they're a captive audience on a long car ride. My children have heard me talk about our long-dead people for so long, they are almost as familiar with the names and the places as I am. When I tell them, *Hey, I found this neat tidbit about Lord Renaud Lempriere,* they'll ask, *Does it involve one of his legitimate kids, or the other one that they called the Bastard of Rozel?* If I say, *Can you hand me that picture of Granny Catherine?* they know exactly which photo on the altar is being referenced. Talk to your living family members and get them involved. Even if they're not ready to delve into ancestor work on a spiritual level, you can still share the history. After all, this is their family too.

Regardless of how much you share with them verbally, good recordkeeping is a must for any genealogical legacy you want to leave behind. Those big piles of photos you have in a box in your closet that you once thought you'd make into scrapbooks should be dug out and labeled, every single one of them. If you don't do this before you die, who will?

I have an entire plastic tote of photos from the late nineteenth and early twentieth centuries. I know which families they're from, because they came from my grandmother's cedar chest after she died. But I'm not sure who a lot of the people in them are. I can identify a few pretty clearly—Great Aunt Rose, because she looks like my own mirror reflection, or her brother Bill, and my grandmother herself and her two sisters. Beyond that, there are a lot of women in long dresses with big hats, and stern looking men with sideburns, and I can't figure out who most of them could be. That makes me a little sad, because I *want* to know them. But no one ever labeled most of the photos, unless it's a small scribbled line, e.g., *The lake house* or *Trip to St. Louis.*

Don't leave a legacy of anonymity behind. Put names and dates and places on those photos. Buy a scanner and digitize things—you should probably be doing this anyway to add them to your genealogy database, remember? When you digitize them, add labels and tags and notes. Who is in the photo? Where are they? When was the picture taken? Include as much information as you can.

One of the most popular genealogy legacy projects out there is a family history book. You can either make it yourself and add to it regularly, in a binder or other organizational system, or you can go fancy and have it printed up and bound. Either way, it's going to make it easy on the next people in your family who come along and want to know the scoop on their ancestral heritage. Think of it as a relay race in the Olympics. You get to pass the baton to the next runner.

When you're chronicling your family tree for the future, be sure to include your notes about the research trails you've followed. Document your sources thoroughly and be sure to even write down your mistakes—that will keep future genealogists in your family from repeating those errors and going down the wrong rabbit hole. Share your successes and your failures.

Keep in mind that if you have young children living with you, talking about your ancestors on a regular basis can help normalize the idea of speaking with them. Saying *Goodnight grandmothers, goodnight grandfathers, goodnight ancestors* on the way past the altar every night can become a bedtime routine when children are younger. By the time they're ready to do ancestor work themselves—or your ancestors decide they want to welcome the newest generation of kinfolk into the practice—speaking to long-dead family members will be nothing out of the ordinary. Including kids in your practice, beliefs, and ritual work is a natural way to share your family's legacy.

Family Heirlooms

Does your family have heirlooms? Mine doesn't have many—we're kind of minimalists—but there are a few really important items I want to leave behind for my kids, and I want them to know the story behind them. One of my most prized possessions is my grandfather's desk. It's six feet wide, three feet deep, and has a roll-top and about a dozen drawers and compartments. It's so big that when we were kids, my brother and I used to play underneath it. It's got a leather blotting pad, and on humid days, I can still get a whiff of my grandfather's pipe tobacco coming off it. It's a wonderful desk, and it came into the family when the company my grandfather worked for decided to upgrade all of their office furniture with fancy new metal desks. He was offered the chance to buy his desk for ten bucks, so he did. It's been in the family ever since. One day, it's going to sit in the home of one of my kids, and I want them to know that it was a ten-dollar desk that's been with us for about seven decades.

Write down the history or provenance of any heirlooms and decide in advance to whom they will go. If you don't have children of your own, talk to siblings and cousins and nieces and nephews. Find out who is going to want what when you die—you don't want to leave your grandmother's good china to someone who's not going to appreciate it, or worse yet, turn around and sell it to the local pawn shop.

Also remember that an heirloom doesn't have to be old. Just because you made or bought something yourself doesn't mean it won't be an heirloom to future generations. Do you quilt or paint or do woodwork? Is there a piece of jewelry or artwork that has special sentimental meaning to you, even though it wasn't in your family until you found it and brought it home? Write down the stories of these items and create your own heirlooms; what matters is not the age of the item, but the importance of the meaning behind it.

If you're not sure what you have that would make a good heirloom legacy, that's okay. Get a box and fill it with small things that are important to you. A photo or two of your children, your engagement ring that doesn't fit any more, the tassel from your college graduation. All of these things that define who you are will help paint a picture of the real you for future generations.

Journals and Diaries

One of the richest sources of information we have about people who lived in the past is their own words. Diaries, journals, and letters have helped shape the way we view history and our ancestors themselves. Ever wish you could find that Civil War diary from your great-something grandfather who marched barefoot from Massachusetts to Georgia? Your descendants might just feel the same way about you, so why not leave them something good to read?

Write down your thoughts, your hopes, and your dreams. Did something interesting happen in the world of culture or politics? Share it and explain how and why it affected you. If something significant took place in your life—you got a promotion at work, or you decided to go back to school at age forty, or you found out you were going to be a dad for the first time—write it down. Whether you hand write these memories in a pretty leather-bound journal, or tap it out on your laptop in the coffee shop, all of these things will one day help your descendants understand you and the world you lived in.

Family Recipes and Traditions

Many of us have a vast repository of memories that surround mealtimes with our family. Put together a collection of recipes that have special significance to you and explain why they're important in your family or culture. Even if you personally don't love to cook—or your children don't—there are still plenty of meals and recipes you can pass along.

Is there a certain dish that's the trademark of your culture? What about that soup from the Old Country that you remember your grandmother making when you were sick as a child? You might not have *her* recipe—old-world grandmothers are notorious for not writing down ingredients—but maybe you can come up with your own version of it. What about those stuffed meatballs your children love to have every Saturday night during fall sports season? Include all of these. Assemble the lists of ingredients, the directions, and photos of what a perfect version of this dish should look like when it's done.

If you're having trouble deciding what foods to include, that's okay—turn it into a family project. Ask other relatives for their own recipe stories, especially the older folks. Find out what foods they ate as children on a regular basis, in their parents' and grandparents' homes, and the memories associated with those dinners or breakfasts. Again, learning about the anthropology of your peoples' food will tell you a lot about how they lived overall. Did they eat fancy cuisine, or did they make do with whatever their land provided? Did they fish and hunt for fresh meat, or live in a place where grain and vegetables were the primary staple of each meal?

Keep in mind that as our ancestors became more mobile, their food and cooking patterns would have shifted as well. You may have a collection of recipes that were originally German, for instance, but then blended with the diet of neighbors in a nearby country. Perhaps you don't care for the cookery of your extended family, but you've adopted the customary foods of the community you live in. Ask any Midwesterner about Green Bean Casserole or Sour Cream Potatoes—they know the recipes by heart, and their kids will too. That's food heritage in action, and you can pass it down.

What other traditions do you have in your family that you'd like to preserve for your future kinfolk? Think about things you do on a regular basis, where each of you knows the routine and the part you play in it. Traditions are actions or customs that are done with purpose. They require some degree of thought or planning, and they're important in providing a source of identity for families. Whether they give you an awareness of your family's religious history—do you always take Grandma to church at midnight on Christmas Eve?—or your cultural heritage—Uncle Seamus serving a haggis and whisky on Burns Night while he recites poetry—a family tradition is something that strengthens the bond between kinfolk.

Your traditions can be simple ones, like having a certain dinner routine every night, or something more complicated. Maybe every year you celebrate the Fourth of July with a big barbecue out at the lake. Everyone knows when it is, and even though Aunt Karen always brings that unseasoned, bland potato salad, no one would miss it for the world. Perhaps a certain date is always celebrated the same way every year. If your loved ones are buried nearby, your family traditions might include designated visits to the cemetery on specific days—birthdays, death anniversaries, or other dates that have meaning.

You might even be doing things already that you don't view as a tradition. In our family, every year on the first Saturday in December, we go out to cut down a tree for the holidays. I didn't even realize it had become so ingrained in our family custom until one year when I pondered *not* doing it and was met with immediate outrage from all three of my offspring. *Mooooommmmm, we ALWAYS get the tree!* (We got the tree.)

Family traditions tend to have other benefits as well. In our hectic and chaotic, non-stop busy lives, a ritualized tradition offers a feeling of comfort. They give us a constant. It's easier to deal with all of the fast-paced stress and variables in our daily activities, if we have things to look forward to that will always be the same, no matter what. *I can handle all these deadlines at work, because Saturday is the big summer breakfast with the cousins …*

Established traditions also allow us to share the values and beliefs that matter to us. Whether you're someone who focuses on education and learning, on spirituality and prayer, or even on simple storytelling, traditions are a way for us to solidify the things that matter to us. They add to the opportunities we have to connect with other generations. Do you remember your parents and grandparents reading to you as a kid? Have you taken a child, niece, or nephew fishing lately? All of these behaviors today will create lasting memories in the future, and your descendants will be able to look back at you fondly, recalling the routine stuff that you did together.

If you don't think your family has traditions, and you want to create new ones, ask yourself what the purpose is. Are you shooting for basic family solidarity, or do you want to instill certain patterns and values in the rest of the clan? Once you've figured out your purpose, examine how you'd like to share it and make it a regular occurrence. Also, don't be afraid to eliminate from your life any traditions that are harmful or unpleasant, or that simply no longer bring a sense of joy and wonder to your family.

Bury a Time Capsule

Have you ever seen news stories about towns that celebrate their centennial or some other auspicious date with the unearthing of a time capsule? The town council gathers in front of the cameras, they dig up a giant metal box, and when they open it, there's all kinds of neat stuff from fifty or a hundred years ago. It's a pretty cool idea, and it gives us great insight into the past.

Why not assemble a family time capsule of your own, for your descendants to open as a legacy some day? Think about some things you can include that will show generations to come what it was like to live in your world. Some things you could place in your time capsule might be:

- Write a letter to your descendants. Let them know your personal story, and that of the people who came before you. Share with them your hopes for the future, and your dreams for them. If you assembled a family history book or photo album, place that in there for them as well.

- Gather newspapers from significant dates in your lifetime. You can add one from the city in which your child was born, on the date of their birth. Did you save your *New York Times* from the morning after 9/11, or the day Barack Obama won the presidential election? What about clippings of events that directly impacted you, like the time you made the local paper because you started a rescue program for shelter dogs?

- Did you save small items from the lives of your kids such as their hospital bracelets or ink prints of their tiny little newborn feet? What about that stuffed Winnie the Pooh from your own childhood? Select a few that are meaningful and add them to your capsule.

- Add coins and curios and stamps that have been issued throughout your lifetime; if you're someone who's a collector of any of these things, put a few of your favorites in there. Are you a superhero fan? Why not add a sheet of those cool Wonder Woman postage stamps? Put in a shiny penny, nickel, dime, and quarter from the year you were born.

To make the actual time capsule, you'll need a box or container that's weather and moisture proof. No one wants to unearth a box full of soggy useless paper in the future; stainless steel is ideal for anything that's going to be buried longer than ten years. You might also want to line your capsule with some acid-free paper, to help keep damage to the contents minimal; it's also a good idea to toss in some of those silica gel packets from your shoeboxes or new purse to help absorb any latent moisture.

If you're going to physically bury your time capsule, there are a couple of things you'll need to be sure of. First, be certain to put it in a place that's never going to be disturbed be developers or contractors digging up a yard. Second, make sure you leave a marker so that your descendants can find it. If you're tech-savvy—and if you're not, ask a teenager for help—you can add GPS coordinates into your will, so that when you're long dead and gone, someone else will be able to track the location of your capsule.

Be sure to leave instructions for your descendants. When do you want them to open your time capsule? Should they wait fifty years? Crack it open on the twentieth anniversary of your death? Tell them when and where to dig it up and open it. If you're not a fan of digging holes or you're someone who moves around a lot and you're concerned that your people might be hundreds of miles away from your capsule when it's time to open it, you can stash it with your personal belongings. Put it in your closet, your attic, the basement, or somewhere else that it will be out of the way yet easy to find once you're gone. Mark it clearly, with a date: *Do not open until December 25, 2068*.

If you want to make things really exciting and interesting for your family, leave them enough money that they can plan a big celebration around the opening of your time capsule.

Plan a Family Reunion

A family reunion is an incredibly powerful way to create a legacy for your kinfolk. If you've been doing your genealogy research, you may have tracked down long-distance cousins, perhaps people with whom your shared ancestor is ten generations back. How wonderful would it be to meet all the people descended from that one person?

I once attended a conference in Atlanta held in a large hotel on the north end of the city. This particular hotel is extremely popular for reunions because it's so big; the weekend I was there, a family was there celebrating their heritage. I had the privilege of talking to two of the organizers, who told me they had more than three hundred people in attendance, some of whom had flown in from places all over the world. Every single one of the people at this reunion was descended from a single common ancestor, eight generations in the past. It was incredibly moving to see the spiritual connection that each and every one of them felt, all rooted in this one individual who had lived and died almost two centuries ago.

Once you've figured out the time and the place for your reunion, it's time to start recruiting help, because you can't do it alone.

Whether you're planning a small cookout at the park with barbecue and water balloon games, or a giant celebration with hundreds of people at a conference center, wearing matching t-shirts and sitting in a banquet hall, you're going to need assistance. Find cousins and other relatives, and delegate tasks to them. This is where your organizational and management skills will come into play—as well as your ability to follow a budget. You can have one person in charge of food, another responsible for travel and lodging arrangements, while someone else organizes the entertainment.

One thing that should be included in every family reunion is storytelling. Enlist various family members to tell stories for posterity and record them. That way, not only do you have these memories for the future, you've got them in the voices of your ancestors. It doesn't even have to be any kind of formal interview session. Think about some of the questions you can ask the elders in your family, framed in the context of fact-finding:

- What was it like when you joined the army and got sent overseas?

- Can you tell me about that visit to your grandfather's farm in Kansas the summer the tornado hit?

- What were the challenges for you, growing up in this country when your parents didn't speak English like your friends' parents did?

Although you can certainly include a list of specific things you want to know about, sometimes it's best just to let the conversation flow organically. You might uncover some buried treasure about a relative's past. Plan on transcribing these recordings later.

If you can store them as digital files with the rest of your geneal-ogy material, even better.

End of Life Planning

No one likes to think about their own mortality. In most of the Western world, we grow up fearing the idea of dying, death itself, and that when we do finally pack it in, we are going to leave loved ones behind to cope with our loss. We've been raised to believe that no matter what our beliefs in the afterlife may be, death is pretty final. One way you can make things just a little bit easier—and possibly bring yourself some relief in the process—is by plan-ning ahead for your own demise.

There are a few very sensible reasons for doing this. First of all, it helps to take a lot of the stressful decision-making off the shoulders of those who love you. When someone dies, particularly if it's unexpected, there are arrangements to be made, caskets to be selected, funerals to be planned, to say nothing of wills and pro-bate and all of the legal drama. For survivors, who may not be in the best emotional state, this process can be terrifying and anxiety inducing. Making as many of these decisions as possible ahead of time will help lighten the mental load for your children, spouse, and other family members.

Another reason to consider end of life planning? Frankly, it alle-viates a lot of the guilt that loved ones often experience when they start second-guessing their own decisions. *What would Mom have really wanted us to do? Do you think this memorial service would fit in with Grandpa's wishes?* Making these choices so that others don't have to is a powerful gift to leave your family members.

Many people discover during end of life planning that map-ping out their wishes and expectations ahead of time helps on an emotional level. Planning in this way takes some of the fear of the unknown out of the equation both for the person doing the planning and for their family. Pre-planning your own funeral or memorial service can turn what might normally be a nightmare into a beautiful celebration of your own life, and that's something all of us can feel pretty good about.

So how do you plan for something as unpredictable as the end of your own life? One of the first things you should do is write out two important documents. The first is called an advance directive, although you may hear it referred to as a living will. This spells out your very specific wishes as far as what sort of medical care you want or don't want, in the event that you yourself are unable to give consent. If I'm in a traumatic accident and lose consciousness, I don't want my kids to have to squabble in a hospital hallway about which heroic measures should be taken to help me. It's right there in black and white, written down what I want done, and what I don't want done. It also includes my wishes that my organs be donated to help anyone who can use them once I can't any longer.

The second document you need to create is a medical power of attorney. This is sometimes referred to as a healthcare proxy, and it designates the person you want to make medical decisions on your behalf when you can't do it. You may want to pick your spouse or child, but a lot of people choose a sibling instead, so that they don't have to put the pressure of making hard choices on a frightened wife, husband, son, or daughter. Both of these documents are things you can have a lawyer prepare for you, but most US states allow you to create your own; it's usually a good idea to get them witnessed and notarized. Be sure to put copies in a safe place and give a copy to family members who will be making these choices for you in the event of a medical tragedy.

Next consider writing a will. Even if you don't have a lot of assets, it's still important to do this. A will allows you to name legal guardians if you have underage children, and it's something you should update any time you have a major life event, like a marriage or divorce, the birth of another child, or even a sudden increase in your own financial status. Your will can also designate someone who can take care of your bank accounts once you're gone. Be sure to share the fact that you've written a will with family members and where they can find it—but don't overshare. You don't want your sister and your daughter bickering for the next three decades because they both want that really snazzy credenza in your living room.

Something else most people don't think about is their digital legacy. If you die, what do you want done with your Facebook page or your Instagram account? Nearly all social media platforms allow you to designate someone who can be your legacy account holder, so be sure to look into that before it's too late. I've designated my oldest daughter and my best friend as my legacy contacts for Facebook, so once I kick off, they can either turn it into a memorial page for me or, with any luck, they'll get to post completely inappropriate memes on my behalf.

One of the parts of end of life planning that people seem to find the most spiritually satisfying is that of deciding what sort of funeral and memorial service they want. Funerals can be expensive, so it's tempting to go ahead and pay for a casket and burial plot in advance—but prices fluctuate, and what if you or your family members end up moving to a new city before you die? Instead, it's a good idea to take the money you would have paid to a funeral home and put it in a separate bank account designated specifically for your funeral expenses. Be sure to make it a joint account with one of your family members, so they can access the funds even when you're dead. If you prefer to do a "green" burial, or a natural burial without chemicals or a casket, be sure to include that in your written list of wishes. Some people even put together a file of things they want at their funeral and leave it in a place where the next of kin can find it easily. Do you hate the smell of gardenias? Can't stand the idea of being buried next to your rotten Aunt Janice? Put all that in your planner, so your family knows there shouldn't be any gardenias—or any Aunt Janice—at your funeral.

Like every other aspect of death planning, arranging your own memorial service is a uniquely personal process. Think about how you want to be remembered. Do you want your service to be a sad and somber occasion with lots of weeping, or a joyful one in which people celebrate your life, and share stories and laughter and happiness? There's no right answer to the question, but it's something to think about in advance. Can you leave money behind to pay for a caterer, a mariachi band, and a juggler, if that's what you want? Consider all of the things you want your memorial service to include—personally, I'd like my survivors to enjoy a kilted bagpiper, a cask of single-malt Glendronach 18, and a really big bonfire—and commit those details in writing to your end of life plan.

Conclusion
PUTTING IT ALL TOGETHER

At some point, a long time ago, one (and likely more) of your badass kinfolk sat and wondered what future generations would think of them. Someone in your bloodline pondered the question of legacy and what it all meant. What kind of mark would they leave on history, and on their descendants throughout the ages? Whether they rode on horseback across the plains of the Midwest, hunted their food on the Serengeti, or lived in a hut somewhere in a cold coastal village, the fact remains that you are the sum total of all of their parts. You are the end result of hundreds of generations of blended DNA.

Some of those people in your gene pool did rotten things; there's no denying it. They may have oppressed other people, perpetuated colonialism, and lived in ways that make us cringe today. Maybe they were criminals, or violent and abusive. Perhaps they just weren't nice at all.

But for every terrible ancestor who lived in the past, there are plenty of good people as well. You had brave, honest, hard-working men and women. You had heroes, even though you may not know who they were. Your family tree includes people who performed wonderful acts of courage and kindness, not because they clamored for recognition or they wanted to go viral on social media, but just because they were in the right place at the right time and chose to do the right thing. In other words, good and bad, they were *people*, and the more you work with them the more you'll come to recognize that.

For some of us, our ancestors are with us all the time. They're badasses, protectors, warriors, the ride-or-die guides we all need in our lives. And that comes as a direct result of making the effort to cultivate a rich and rewarding relationship with our people. Whether you're calling on an individual nestled in far-off and obscure branches of the family tree, the great-grandmother you knew since childhood, or the collective whole, your ancestral guides can step in and bring you power and wisdom and strength in ways that you've never experienced before.

Ancestral work isn't easy—that's why it's called *work* and not Ancestral Playtime—and it can be emotionally draining at times, but it's definitely rewarding for those who want to put the effort into it. Your people can help you get past feelings of helplessness or betrayal. They can show you how to move towards healing and empowerment and control over your own life. Your people can guide you as you learn to be courageous through your own vulnerability. They're not out there waiting to punish you for your mistakes; instead, they want you to see every possible opportunity for growth, success, and happiness.

By inviting your ancestors into your life as guides, you'll be able to attain a certain degree of spiritual freedom—because these are the people who can help you unpack and address your trauma, give you the strength to stand up for who you are, and the wisdom to live authentically. They'll point you towards success, both the material kind and the spiritual kind, because our ancestors want us to live well. They want you to be prosperous. They want you to bring honor and pride to your bloodlines.

They want you to be a badass, just like they were. What are you waiting for?

Appendix
GENEALOGY RESOURCES

Charts, Forms, and Tables

Want to get started organizing your people into simple charts that will help you keep track of who your badass ancestors were, when they did stuff, and who their parents were? Use an Ahnentafel chart to keep track of things as you begin gathering information. Start with yourself at position 1, your parents at 2 and 3, and so on. You can even create additional pedigree charts for other people on your sheet—let's say you've discovered the ancestors of your maternal great-grandmother, who sits at 15 on your chart. Begin a new chart with her at the #1 position and carry on from there.

There are plenty of places online that you can find an Ahnentafel chart—they're usually free to download—and the style you use is going to be a matter of personal preference. Websites such as www.GenealogySearch.org and www.FamilySearch.org have wonderful templates that you can download and fill out to your heart's content, going back several generations. The grand master of all genealogy websites, Ancestry.com, has Ahnentafel charts and doesn't require paid membership to use them; on that site they're referred to as Ancestry Charts but other websites call them Pedigree Charts—they're all essentially the same thing.

You can also create Family Group Sheets to help sort through which parents had which children. If the couple had more offspring than you can fit on one Family Group Sheet, that's okay—simply use extra sheets and adjust the number for each kid accordingly. Be sure to record your sources—write down where you found information when you locate it. Note down whether it was a census record, a birth certificate, a family bible, et cetera.

For standard Family Group Sheets, again, you'll find some of the best and easiest to use versions at GenealogySearch.org, Family Search.org, and Ancestry.com. In addition to these forms, Ancestry also has a number of other useful templates in their Free Charts and Forms sections—use their Research Calendar sheet to account for all of the sources you've looked at and when you viewed them, the Research Extract form to summarize long and tedious collections of information into a practical selection of important facts, and their Correspondence Record to keep track of all of the various kinfolk, websites, and historical archives contacts that you've gotten in touch with to ask questions about your heritage

Online Resources

Ancestor work can be research-intensive. Consider using some of these free resources for online research in the United States.

- Use Family Search for free research of digitized collections like census records, burial records, and more. This site also allows you to connect with other researchers who are hunting for the same family members. www.familysearch.org.

- HeritageQuest Online is free to try from your home computer courtesy of your library card via participating institutions. HeritageQuest is "powered by," although not directly owned by, Ancestry.com. This partnership has expanded its half-dozen collections to a lighter version of Ancestry, including the complete US census, military and immigration records, and city directories. Click Search and scroll all the way to the bottom to unlock more US records as well as selected foreign databases. www.heritagequestonline .com/hqoweb/library/do/login.

• Check out the Library of Congress. Though not specifically focused on genealogy, the nation's library has plenty to offer online, including the National Union Catalog of Manuscript Collections, the American Memory collection, and its own comprehensive catalog. loc.gov/.

• Explore the National Archives and Records Administration. You can read all about the genealogical treasures stored at the National Archives, order military and other historical records, and browse maps and photos. The National Archives Databases include files ranging from World War enlistments to passenger lists for millions of immigrants from Germany, Ireland, Italy, and Russia, among others. aad.archives.gov/aad/.

• The volunteer site USGenWeb, recently celebrated its twentieth birthday, and its state and county pages are even more useful than ever. Just found an ancestor who lived in, say, Jackson County, Georgia? There's a page for that, as for almost every other place your family may have landed. usgenweb.org/.

• The Ellis Island & Statue of Liberty Foundation has millions of passenger and immigration records. Although not all immigrants came through Ellis Island, if there's a chance yours did, it's a wealth of resources to get you started on your search. libertyellisfoundation.org/passenger.

- Cyndi's List is a massive collection of genealogy websites that you can access, covering over a quarter of a million different links, all categorized and cross-referenced in nearly a hundred different categories. Cyndislist.com.

Enslaved Ancestors Research

If you've reached a brick wall in trying to research an ancestor who was enslaved in the United States, you're going to have to dig a little deeper. Because of the nature of the institution of chattel slavery, researching enslaved ancestors presents a unique set of circumstances that doesn't apply when you're researching people who came to the United States of their own volition. The resources in this list are specifically curated to help people of African heritage trace their enslaved ancestors.

Please be aware that the chattel slavery inflicted upon Africans in the colonial era is *not* the same as the indentured servitude that some white Irish and English people experienced; for resources on indentures, check the next section.

- The Digital Library on American Slavery is a free resource hosted by the University of North Carolina at Greensboro. This database includes digitized details about American slaves drawn from thousands of court and legislative petitions filed in more than a dozen states between 1775 and 1867. library.uncg.edu/slavery/.

- Tom Blake has spent many years identifying the largest slaveholders within the 1860 U.S. census and matching those surnames to African American households listed in the 1870 census, which was the first federal census to list former slaves by name rather than simply as a quantity. Blake estimates that these large slaveholders held as much as 30 percent of the total number of slaves in the United States in 1860. His website, Large Slaveholders of 1860, is at: freepages.rootsweb.com/~ajac/genealogy/.

• The Southern Claims Commission, while not specifically focused on slavery or African Americans, is a rich source of surprising details about people living in the southern United States. These records include the names and ages of many formerly enslaved people, their places of residence, names of owners, manumission records, ownership of property by enslaved people, conditions faced by free Black people, and a great deal of first-person background information on what it was like to be African-American during both the colonial period and after the Civil War. www .fold3.com/category/27/southern-claims-commission.

• At the Trans-Atlantic Slave Trade Database, you can search by voyage, examine estimates of the slave trade, or search a database of more than ninety thousand Africans taken from captured slave ships or from African trading sites. www.slavevoyages.org/.

• The African Origins website has information about the migration histories of Africans forcibly carried onto slave ships across the Atlantic, and compiles geographic, ethnic, and linguistic data on peoples taken from Africa. www .african-origins.org/.

• There are numerous county and state resources in places like Virginia, North Carolina, and Tennessee, and a bit of creative internet searching will yield plenty of results.

Just key in a Google search for "slave genealogy [state]" or "slave records [state]".

- Other databases that include things like African American sailors and soldiers from the Civil War can sometimes give insight to the names and locations of people who were previously enslaved and then later became free.

Indentured Servant Research

Indentured servitude was the way many people solved the problem of the exorbitant expense of migrating from their homelands to the new world of colonial America. It's estimated that as many as 65 percent of the European people who came to the colonies prior to the American Revolution were able to do so because they signed some sort of indenture or work contract. An indenture typically lasted five to seven years, and the person—and sometimes their family, too—worked in exchange for passage. In some cases, indentures were a way to get out of criminal sentencing. Once the contract was up, they were given the freedom to go on about their business, own land, and do all the other things free people did in a fledgling nation.

If your ancestors were indentured servants—*not* enslaved individuals, (again, a whole different thing)—there are a couple of really wonderful online resources you can access that will provide information to help you get started.

- A professional genealogy firm in Utah, Price & Associates, offers a free searchable database of thousands of indentured servant records. It's still an ongoing project, but it covers immigration as far back as 1630 up through 1820. The firm's goal is to eventually have information on as

many as 100,000 indentured immigrants. www.pricegen
.com/immigrantservants/search/simple.php

- Search county and local historical archives for documents
such as apprenticeship bonds and servant registers.

- Jamestown, Virginia, is one of the earliest settlements in
America, and was the home of thousands of immigrants
from Britain and its neighboring countries. The Virtual
Jamestown website has a free database that contains about
15,000 indentured servitude records spanning the second
half of the seventeenth century. These records cover
more than just Jamestown itself—if your people settled
in Virginia, it's a great resource—and includes some great
reference articles about the laws behind indenture, and
newspaper postings about runaway servants. www.virtual
jamestown.org/

- The late British genealogist Peter Wilson Coldham worked
at the British Public Records Office and frequently found
references to American colonists among the records. He
ended up publishing more than two dozen books about
indenture and British migration to America, which
included paid servitude and convict transportation. His
Complete Book of Emigrants 1607–1660 is one of a series that
breaks down immigration by time period, from England to
America, and Coldham's transcription of *The Lord Mayor's
Court in London: Dispositions Relating to Americans 1641–1735*
covers court cases that include indentures, as well as land
grants and merchant disputes.

- The New Early Settlers of Maryland website includes a
database of nearly 35,000 immigrants who arrived in the
colony between 1634 and 1681. Maryland had a system

called *headrights* for land distribution, which meant that one could obtain fifty acres of land for each person transported. This system made Maryland prime ground for wealthy people who wanted to acquire land and were willing to buy indenture contracts. earlysettlers.msa.maryland.gov/.

Books Every Genealogist Should Read

As you dive into online databases, it's easy to get lost in the endless webs of information, so sometimes it's great to get back to the basics. These are three books that anyone serious about their family history should read at some point.

- *Who Do You Think You Are?* by Megan Smolenyak (Penguin Books, 2010). This is the book that serves as a companion guide to the hit television show of the same name and includes detailed yet easy-to-understand resources on all kinds of topics. Whether you're trying to figure out how to archive an old photo, decipher a strange word on a census record, or get new ideas for places to search, this book is perfect for beginners and veterans alike.

- *The Everything Guide to Online Genealogy* by Kimberly Powell (Everything Press, 2011) is exactly what it sounds like! Don't be intimidated—it's chock-full of tips on online resources, search keywords to try out, and how to connect with other researchers on the internet and social media.

- *The Source: A Guidebook of American Genealogy,* edited by Loretto Dennis Szucs and Sandra Hargreaves Luebking (Ancestry Publishing, 2006), is a monster at almost a thousand pages. This is *the* book that a lot of professional researchers swear by—it's the quintessential guide to identifying and locating both primary and secondary sources, and it contains content written by some three dozen experts in the field of family history research.

Other books that would be helpful to have on hand include local histories to help you learn about the places your badass ancestors lived, religious tomes, political guides, and even—if you're lucky enough to find it—other people's published genealogical studies of your family. Do you have an ancestor who was a member of a prominent family? Get your hands on books that detail that family's history and provenance—if you can trace your line back to royalty, this information is recorded in meticulous historical detail. If someone in your family did something that made them famous—for good or bad—pick up biographies, which may reveal more clues as to who else they were related to.

BIBLIOGRAPHY

Callaway, Ewen. "Most Europeans Share Recent Ancestors."
Nature News. Nature Publishing Group. https://www.nature
.com/news/most-europeans-share-recent-ancestors-1.12950.

Fery, George. "The Day of the Dead in Mexico." George Fery–
Freelance Writer & Photographer of the New World and
Mesoamerica, October 29, 2019. https://www.georgefery.
com/day
-of-the-dead.

Gross, David K. "Shamanism and the State: A Conflict Theory
Perspective." ScholarWorks at University of Montana. https://
scholarworks.umt.edu/etd/5552.

Herrmann, Virginia Rimmer., J. David Schloen, and Anna R. Ress-
man. *In Remembrance of Me: Feasting with the Dead in the Ancient
Middle East*. Chicago: Oriental Institute of the University of
Chicago, 2014.

Huamán Poma de Ayala, Don Felipe, and Christopher Dilke. *Letter to a King: a Peruvian Chiefs Account of Life under the Incas and
under Spanish Rule*. New York: Dutton, 1978.

"Irish-Catholic Immigration. Classroom Presentation: Teacher Resources." Library of Congress. http://www.loc.gov/teachers /classroommaterials/presentationsandactivities/presentations /immigration/irish2.html.

Lerner, Louise. "Ancient Urban Villa with Shrine for Ancestor Worship Discovered in Egypt." University of Chicago News. https://news.uchicago.edu/story/ancient-urban-villa-shrine -ancestor-worship-discovered-egypt.

Kuijt, Ian. "Place, Death, and the Transmission of Social Memory in Early Agricultural Communities of the Near Eastern Pre-Pottery Neolithic." *Archeological Papers of the American Anthropological Association* 10, no. 1 (2008): 80–99.

Malinowski, Bronislaw. "Magic, Science and Religion." *Death, Mourning and Burial: A Cross-Cultural Reader*, 2004, 19–22.

McClintock, Walter. *Old North Trail: Life, Legends and Religion of the Blackfeet Indians (Classic Reprint)*. London: Forgotten Books, 2015.

McCoy, Daniel. "Ancestors." Norse Mythology for Smart People. https://norse-mythology.org/gods-and-creatures/ancestors/.

McCoy, Renee. "African American Elders, Cultural Traditions, and the Family Reunion." African American Elders, Cultural Traditions, and the Family Reunion | American Society on Aging. https://www.asaging.org/blog/african-american-elders -cultural-traditions-and-family-reunion.

Miller, Randall Martin, and John David Smith. *Dictionary of Afro-American Slavery*. Westport, CT: Praeger, 1997.

Morgan, John D., Pittu Laungani, and Stephen Palmer. *Death and Bereavement around the World: Death and Bereavement in the Americas*. Amityville, NY: Baywood Publishing, 2003.

Pauketat, Timothy R. *The Oxford Handbook of North American Archaeology*. New York: Oxford University Press, 2015.

Peoples, Hervey C., Pavel Duda, and Frank W. Marlowe. "Hunter-Gatherers and the Origins of Religion." *Human Nature* 27, no. 3 (June 2016): 261–282.

"Religions—Paganism: Britain's Spiritual History." BBC, April 11, 2008. https://www.bbc.co.uk/religion/religions/paganism/history/spiritualhistory_1.shtml.

Steadman, Lyle B., Craig T. Palmer, and Christopher F. Tilley. "The Universality of Ancestor Worship." *Ethnology* 35, no. 1 (1996): 63.

Torrance, Robert. *Spiritual Quest: Transcendence in Myth, Religion, and Science*. University of California Press, December 5, 2014: 61–99.

"Tzedakah 101." My Jewish Learning. www.myjewishlearning.com/article/tzedakah-101/.

"Were Your Ancestors Indentured Servants? Here's How to Find Out." Family History Daily, May 14, 2018. https://familyhistorydaily.com/free-genealogy-resources/indentured-servants/.

Winkelman, Michael. "Shamanism in Cross-Cultural Perspective." *International Journal of Transpersonal Studies* 31, no. 2 (January 2012): 47–62.

INDEX

A

Abundance, 15, 19, 21, 87, 96, 109, 110, 141, 154

Adoption, 6, 8, 57–60, 121, 127, 139, 205

African Traditional Religions, 20, 64

Ahnentafel Chart, 27, 28, 32, 219

Altar or shrine, 6, 9, 13, 14, 17, 18, 59, 61–77, 79–82, 89–91, 95, 96, 103, 105–107, 110, 111, 114, 117–121, 124, 128, 130–132, 134, 135, 140–143, 145, 146, 155, 168, 170, 172–175, 178, 180, 186, 197, 198, 200, 201, 230

Ancestor veneration, 8, 11, 12, 17–19, 21, 22

Ancestors of the heart, 140

Ancestral foods, 13, 17, 124, 183, 184, 204

Ancestry.com, 26, 27, 37, 219–221

Ancient Egypt, 14

Ancient Greece, 151

Ancient Rome, 13, 164

Archetypes, 6, 9, 58, 59, 93, 102, 139, 147, 148, 151–153, 156–158, 160, 162

B

Baked apples, 195, 197

Baked spaghetti squash, 191

Banishing, 132, 133

Birth certificates, 32–36, 39–41, 132, 220

Bone divination, 180

Broth soup, 187–188

Buddhism, 18, 75, 87

Burial records, 220

C

Candles, 15, 16, 71, 72, 74, 96, 105–107, 114–124, 132–135, 137, 140, 143–146, 170, 171

Census records, 25, 27, 33–35, 37–39, 42, 53, 220–223, 226

Chicken and couscous, 193

D

Dahomey Kingdom, 21–22

Death certificates, 35, 41, 48, 132

Digital photos, 45, 175, 201

Divination, 81, 94, 167, 168, 171, 173, 175–181

Draft card, 46

E

Early period, 12

Eastern spiritualty, 18

Ellis Island, 44, 51–53, 68, 221

Empowerment, 1, 9, 10, 163, 216

End of life planning, 211, 213, 214

Enslaved ancestors, 5, 20, 22, 50, 51, 134, 155, 157, 188, 222–224, 230

Explorer archetype, 160, 161

F

Family bible, 46, 47, 220

Family group sheet, 220

Family reunion, 21, 130, 209, 210, 230

Family Tree Maker, 35

Father and king archetype, 5, 16, 21, 22, 54, 70, 100, 101, 108, 112, 147, 156–158, 160, 161, 164, 229

First Nations, 70

Flowers, 13, 15, 18, 19, 74, 77–81, 114, 117, 118, 122, 143, 144

Forgotten dead, 144, 145

G

Gender norms, 97

Genealogy, 4, 8, 25–27, 35, 36, 39, 43, 66, 108, 199, 201, 209, 211, 219, 221–224, 226

Germanic tribes, 17, 176

Gratitude, 19, 68, 105, 107, 111, 114–116, 120, 121, 144, 181

H

Headstone rubbing, 49, 76

Healing, 2, 16, 23, 82, 90, 91, 99, 116–118, 131, 134–137, 143, 145, 154, 181, 216

Heirlooms, 68, 69, 91, 130, 202

Herbal butter, 191–193

Historical figures, 100, 147, 153

Homestead Act of 1862, 50

I

Incense, 13, 18, 19, 78–81, 92, 105, 117, 119, 140, 143, 145

J

Journals and diaries, 73, 168, 203, 231

K

Katumuwa, 12

L

Lares, 13

Lover archetype, 163, 164

M

Marriage records, 39, 42

Meditation, 59, 81, 92, 93, 105, 112, 113

Memorial box, 74

Mesoamerica, 15, 16, 229

Mesopotamia, 12, 13, 157

Mexico, 15, 17, 20, 197, 229

Middle East, 12, 229

Money, 7, 86, 96, 108–111, 209, 213, 214

Mother and queen archetype, 68, 153, 154, 156, 164

N

Name changes, 51

National Archives, 30, 37, 38, 44, 45, 221

Native Americans, 134

Naturalization records, 44, 45

Norse society, 17–18, 176

O

Obituaries, 48, 49, 74

Offerings, 9, 12, 13, 15–19, 21–23, 72, 119–121, 142

Oracle cards, 173, 175, 181

P

Parentalia, 13, 14

Parentes, 13

Passenger lists, 44, 52, 221, 222

Pendulum, 171–173

Pepper pot stew, 188

Photos, 15, 26, 27, 35, 58, 67, 71, 73, 91, 132, 140,
    174, 175, 199–201, 204, 221

Prayer beads, 75

Prayers, 12, 14, 16, 17, 21, 62, 73, 75, 77, 78, 96, 97,
    103, 107, 123, 124, 184, 197, 206

Problem ancestors, 131, 132, 153

Protection, 2, 18, 23, 61, 80–82, 91, 95, 97, 103–
    105, 128, 152, 154, 177

R

Rebel archetype, 161, 162

Ritual, 13, 21, 61, 62, 66, 67, 75, 79, 88, 103, 104,
    108–110, 114, 116–119, 121, 122, 128, 132, 135,
    137, 140, 143–145, 170, 201

Roots a la crème, 190

Runes, 175–178

S

Sage and crone archetype, 148, 149

Scrying, 168–171, 181

Seasonal greens, 194

Shinto, 18, 75

Silent supper, 122, 123, 197

Social Security Death Index, 41, 42

Soul cakes, 197, 198

Spirit guides, 91, 92

Spiritual ancestors, 5, 18, 22, 60, 69, 96, 139, 142, 143, 148, 200, 216

Staves, 175, 177, 178

T

Time capsule, 207–209

Trauma, 2, 90, 119, 134–137, 181, 216

Trickster archetype, 158, 159

V

Vesta, 13

W

Warrior archetype, 147, 151, 152

West Africa, 70

Wills, 41, 128, 211

To Write to the Author

If you wish to contact the author or would like more information about this book, please write to the author in care of Llewellyn Worldwide Ltd. and we will forward your request. Both the author and publisher appreciate hearing from you and learning of your enjoyment of this book and how it has helped you. Llewellyn Worldwide Ltd. cannot guarantee that every letter written to the author can be answered, but all will be forwarded. Please write to:

Patti Wigington
℅ Llewellyn Worldwide
2143 Wooddale Drive
Woodbury, MN 55125-2989

Please enclose a self-addressed stamped envelope for reply,
or $1.00 to cover costs. If outside the U.S.A., enclose
an international postal reply coupon.

Many of Llewellyn's authors have websites with additional information and resources. For more information, please visit our website at http://www.llewellyn.com